THE
DELL BOOK
OF
LOGIC
PROBLEMS #3

THE
DELL BOOK
OF
LOGIC
PROBLEMS #3

Editor-in-Chief • Erica L. Rothstein
Special Editor • Kathleen Reineke
Editor • Theresa Turner

A DELL TRADE PAPERBACK

A DELL TRADE PAPERBACK

Published by
Dell Publishing
a division of
The Bantam Doubleday Dell Publishing Group, Inc.
666 Fifth Avenue
New York, New York 10103

ISBN: 0-440-50068-0

Printed in the United States of America
Published simultaneously in Canada

November 1988

10 9 8 7 6 5 4 3 2 1

MV

A WORD ABOUT THIS BOOK

Welcome to THE DELL BOOK OF LOGIC PROBLEMS #3.

Why are Logic Problems such fun to solve? Perhaps it is because they are so self-contained—no prior knowledge is really necessary to solve a Problem—everything you need to know is contained in the clues. You don't have to carry around a dictionary or consult the encyclopedia for information needed to complete a puzzle. However, even the simplest Problem poses a challenge—the challenge of using the clues given to form conclusions which eventually lead to the solution. For those of you who are new to Logic Problem solving, the easy puzzles are a good way to master the basic skills of solving. The Easy section of this book begins on page 27.

For those of you who already are Logic Problem fans—well, you have already experienced the feeling of accomplishment that is yours when you have successfully pieced together all the variables put forth in the clues. Even Sherlock Holmes couldn't have done a better job! For you, the pages of this book hold the opportunity of sharpening those solving skills even further.

To aid solvers at all skill levels in the complete mastery of Logic Problems, beginning on page 15 of this book you will find invaluable information on the use of solving charts and some "insights into the thought processes that go into solving these puzzles." This step-by-step how-to guide is not only for first-time solvers. Even veteran solvers might glean the answer to some previous "mystery."

The Problems in this book are arranged in sections which proceed from the easiest to the most challenging. Each puzzle has been selected with you the solver in mind. The 75 brand-new puzzles contained herein have been created especially for you by the world's top Logic Problem constructors to bring you the best in Logic Problem entertainment and hours of stimulating, challenging solving fun.

And now, without further ado, we want to wish you happy solving. Remember, all comments, both pro and con, are welcome and will receive considered attention. Write to:

THE EDITORS
Dell Book of Logic Problems #3
Dell Publishing
245 Park Avenue
New York, New York 10167

A LETTER FROM THE EDITOR

Although Logic Problems are now one of my favorite features, it was not always so. When this fledgling editor came on the scene (more years ago than I would care to relate here), Logic Problems were truly a puzzle to me, the subject of many discussions concerning the extraordinary cerebral ability of the constructors of these perplexing problems. In those days (they seem practically prehistoric to me now), Logic Problems were not a regular feature, but rather a once-in-a-while treat. Knowing that I was not lacking in brain power (after all, I was hired as an assistant editor by the world's foremost puzzle publications), I dedicated many hours of fun and frustration, on the job and off, to the solution of my Logic Problem problem. I was certainly not alone in my dedication—I was solving side by side with all of you, learning all we could about this "upstart" in the field of puzzle entertainment and loving every minute of it.

Today, this "upstart" has become one of the most popular features of the Dell puzzle magazines and at least one appears in virtually every issue. But even this relative abundance is not enough to satisfy the voracious appetite of Logic Problem fans—hence the inauguration of this series.

This is the third paperback book devoted entirely to Logic Problems and, to give credit where it is due, this series owes its existence to the amazing foresight of Editor-in-Chief Kathleen Rafferty, who, about 15 years ago, told me to start collecting brand-new material for a possible book devoted solely to Logic Problems. Although I got to work immediately, her plan didn't come to fruition until years later, when, in 1984, the first in this very successful series was published.

This book is dedicated to the memory of Kathleen Rafferty, editor extraordinaire, who died in 1981. Kathleen Rafferty was an inspired editor whose expertise in the field of puzzles and her love of and respect for the solver has been passed down to everyone who was lucky enough to come under her tutelage. Her high expectations inspired each and every one of us to strive toward perfecting our own editorial skills. I feel privileged to be a part of her professional heritage.

KATHLEEN REINEKE
Special Editor
Dell Puzzle Publications

CONTENTS

EASY LOGIC PROBLEMS

MEDIUM LOGIC PROBLEMS

HARD LOGIC PROBLEMS

CHALLENGER LOGIC PROBLEMS

THE
DELL BOOK
OF
LOGIC
PROBLEMS #3

HOW TO SOLVE LOGIC PROBLEMS

For those of you who are new to Logic Problems: On the following pages you will find some insights into the thought processes that go into solving these puzzles, as well as detailed instructions on the use of charts as solving aids. We suggest you scan these instructions to familiarize yourself with the techniques presented here. Whenever you feel that you're ready to try your hand at solving, turn to the first puzzle (which you will find on page 27) and dig right in. If, even after you have studied these instructions, you should find yourself stuck while solving, turn to the solution for that puzzle and try to follow the reasoning given there. The solutions are not just a listing of "who did what," but rather a step-by-step elimination of possibilities, which you should find invaluable on your journey along the road to mastery of Logic Problems.

The 75 Logic Problems in this book are just that—problems based on logic, to which you need bring no specialized knowledge of extensive vocabulary. Instead, all you will need is your common sense, some reasoning power, and a basic grasp of how to use the charts or other solving aids provided. The problems themselves are all classic deduction problems, in which you are usually asked to figure out how two or more sets of facts relate to each other—what first name belongs with which last name, for example. All of the facts you will need to solve each puzzle are always given.

The puzzles are mostly arranged in increasing order of difficulty—the first few are rather easy to solve, then the puzzles get more difficult as you continue through the book. The final puzzles are especially challenging. If you are new to Logic Problems, we suggest that you start with the first puzzles, progressing through the book as you get more expert at solving.

Of the three examples which follow, the first is, of course, the most basic, but the skills utilized there will help you tackle even the most challenging challenger. Example #2 will help you hone those skills and gives valuable hints about the use of a more complicated chart as a solving aid. The third member of the group will introduce those puzzles for which the normal solving chart is not applicable. You will notice that in each of these examples, as in all the Logic Problems in this book, the last part of the introduction will tell you what facts you are to establish in solving that puzzle. Now, if you are ready to begin, read through the introduction and the clues given with Example #1.

EXAMPLE #1

A young woman attending a party was introduced to four men in rather rapid succession and, as usual at such gatherings, their respective types of work were mentioned rather early in the conversation. Unfortunately, she was afflicted with a somewhat faulty memory. Half an hour later, she could remember only that she had met a Mr. Brown, a Mr. White, a Mr. Black, and a Mr. Green. She recalled that among them were a photographer, a grocer, a banker, and a singer, but she could not recall which was which. Her hostess, a fun-loving friend, refused to refresh her memory, but offered four clues. Happily, the young woman's logic was better than her memory, and she quickly paired each man with his profession. Can you? Here are the clues:

1. Mr. White approached the banker for a loan.

2. Mr. Brown had met the photographer when he hired him to take pictures of his wedding.

3. The singer and Mr. White are friends, but have never had business dealings.

4. Neither Mr. Black nor the singer had ever met Mr. Green before that evening.

	Black	Brown	Green	White
banker				X
grocer				
photo.		X		
singer				

You know from the last part of the introduction what it is you are to determine—you are to match each man's last name with his profession. The chart has been set up to help you keep track of the information as you discover it. We suggest that you use an X in a box to indicate a definite impossibility and a • (dot) in a box to show an established fact.

Your first step is to enter X's into the chart for all of the obvious possibilities that you can see from information given in the clues. It is apparent from clue 1 that Mr. White is not the banker, so an X would be entered into the White/banker box. Clue 2 makes it clear that Mr. Brown is not the photographer, so another X in the Brown/photographer box can be entered. Clue 3 tells you that Mr. White is not the singer. And from clue 4 you can see that neither Mr. Black nor Mr. Green is the singer. Each of these impossibilities should also be indicated by X's in the chart. Once you have done so, your chart will look like this:

	Black	Brown	Green	White
banker				X
grocer				
photo.		X		
singer	X		X	X

Remembering that each X indicates that something is *not* a fact, note the row of boxes at the bottom—corresponding to which of the men is the singer. There are four possibilities, and you have X's for three of them. Therefore, Mr. Brown, the only one left, has to be the singer. Put a dot (•) in the singer/Brown box. Also, remember that if Mr. Brown is the singer, he is not the photographer (which we knew, we have an X); and he cannot be the grocer or the banker either. Thus, you would put X's in those boxes too. Your chart would now look like this:

	Black	Brown	Green	White
banker		X		X
grocer		X		
photo.		X		
singer	X	•	X	X

Now you seem to have a "hopeless" situation! You have used all the clues, and you have matched one man with his profession—but the additional X's entered in the chart do not enable you to make another match, since the possibilities have not been narrowed down sufficiently. What to do next?

Your next step is to reread the clues, at the same time considering the new information you have acquired: You know that Mr. Brown is the singer and that he has done business with the photographer (clue 2). But the singer has never done business with Mr. White (clue 3) or with Mr. Green (clue 4). And that means that neither Mr. White nor Mr. Green can possibly be the photographer. You can now place X's in those boxes in the chart. After you have done so, here is what you will have:

	Black	Brown	Green	White
banker		X		X
grocer		X		
photo.		X	X	X
singer	X	•	X	X

And you see that you do have more answers! The photographer must be Mr. Black, since there are X's in the boxes for the other names. Mr. White, also, must be the grocer, since there is an X in the other three boxes under his name. Once you have placed a dot to indicate that Mr. Black is the photographer and a dot to show that Mr. White is the grocer (always remembering to place X's in the other boxes in the row and column that contain the dot) your chart will look like this:

	Black	Brown	Green	White
banker	X	X		X
grocer	X	X	X	•
photo.	•	X	X	X
singer	X	•	X	X

You can see that you are left with one empty box, and this box corresponds to the remaining piece of information you have not yet determined—what Mr. Green's profession is and who the banker is. Obviously, the only possibility is that Mr. Green is the banker. And the Logic Problem is solved!

Most of the Logic Problems in this book will ask you to determine how more than two sets of facts are related to each other. You'll see, however, that the way of solving a more involved Logic Problem is just the same as Example #1—*if* you have a grasp of how to make the best use of the solving chart. The next example of a Logic Problem is presented in order to explain how to use a bigger chart. As before, read through the problem quickly, noting that the introduction tells you what facts you are to determine.

EXAMPLE #2

Andy, Chris, Noel, Randy, and Steve—one of whose last name is Morse—were recently hired as refreshment vendors at Memorial Stadium; each boy sells only one kind of fare. From the clues below, try to determine each boy's full name and the type of refreshment he sells.

1. Randy, whose last name is not Wiley, does not sell popcorn.

2. The Davis boy does not sell soda or candy.

3. The five boys are Noel, Randy, the Smith boy, the Coble boy, and the boy who sells ice cream.

4. Andy's last name is not Wiley or Coble. Neither Andy nor Coble is the boy who sells candy.

5. Neither the peanut vendor nor the ice cream vendor is named Steve or Davis.

	Coble	Davis	Morse	Smith	Wiley	candy	ice.	pean.	pop.	soda
Andy										
Chris										
Noel										
Randy										
Steve										
candy					
ice.					
pean.					
pop.					
soda					

Note that the chart given is composed of three sets of boxes—one set corresponding to the first and last names; a second set (to the right) corresponding to first names and refreshment; and a third set, below the first set, corresponding to the refreshment and last names. Notice, too, that these sets are separated from each other by heavier lines so that it is easier to find the particular box you are looking for.

As in Example #1, your first step is to enter into the boxes of the chart the impossibilities. Keep in mind that you have many more boxes to be concerned with here. Remember, ROW indicates the boxes that go horizontally (the Andy row, for example) and the word COLUMN indicates the boxes that go vertically (the Coble column, for instance).

Clue 1 tells you that Randy's last name is not Wiley, and Randy does not sell popcorn. Thus, enter an X into the Randy/Wiley box and another X in the Randy/popcorn box in the Randy row. Clue 2 says that the Davis boy sells neither soda nor candy. Find Davis and go down that column to the Davis/soda box and put an X in it; then find the Davis/candy box in that same column and place an X in that box.

Clue 3 tells you a few things: It gives you all five of the boys, either by his first name (two of them), his last name (another two of them), or by what refreshment he sells (the remaining boy). You then know something about all five—one boy's first name is Noel, another's is Randy; a third boy has the last name Smith, a fourth has the last name Coble; and the fifth sells ice cream. All of these are different people. So, in the chart you have a lot of X's that can be entered. Noel's last name is neither Smith nor Coble, so enter X's in the Noel/Smith, Noel/Coble boxes; nor can Noel be the ice cream seller, so put an X in the Noel/ice cream box. Randy is neither Smith nor Coble, and Randy does not sell ice cream, so put the X's in the Randy/Smith, Randy/Coble, and Randy/ice cream boxes. And neither Smith nor Coble sells ice cream, so enter an X in those two boxes.

Clue 4 tells you that Andy's last name is neither Wiley nor Coble. It also says that Andy does not sell candy and neither does the Coble boy. By now you probably know where to put the X's—in the Andy/Wiley box, the Andy/Coble box, the Andy/candy box, and in the box in the Coble column corresponding to candy. From clue 5 you learn that neither Steve nor Davis is the boy who sells either peanuts or ice cream. (One important point here—read clue 5 again, and note that this clue does *not* tell you whether or not Steve's last name is Davis; it tells you only that neither the peanut seller nor the ice cream vendor has the first name Steve or the last name Davis.) Your chart should now look like this:

	Coble	Davis	Morse	Smith	Wiley	candy	ice.	pean.	pop.	soda
Andy	X	✕	✕	↞	＼ X	＼ X				
Chris	✕	✕	✕	✕	◦	✕	▪	✕	✕	✕
Noel	＼ X	◦	✕	＼ X	✕		＼ X			
Randy	＼ X	✕	◦	＼ X	＼ X		＼ X		＼ X	
Steve	◦	✕	✕	✕	✕		X	X		
candy	＼ X	X			✕					
ice.	＼ X	X＼	✕	＼ X	▪					
pean.		X＼			✕					
pop.	✕	✕	✕	✕	✕					
soda		X＼			✕					

From this point on, we suggest that you fill in the above chart yourself as you read how the facts are established. If you look at the Davis column, you will see that you have X's in four of the refreshment boxes; the Davis boy is the one who sells popcorn. Put a dot in the Davis/popcorn box. Now, since it is Davis who sells popcorn, none of the other boys does, so you will put X's in all of the other boxes in that popcorn row.

Your next step will be to look up at the other set of refreshment boxes and see what first names already have an X in the popcorn column. Note that Randy has an X in the popcorn column (from clue 1). Thus, if you know that Randy does not sell popcorn, you now know that his last name is not Davis, since Davis is the popcorn seller. You can then put an X in the Randy/Davis box. After you've done this, you'll see that you now have four X's for Randy's last name. Randy has to be Morse, the only name left, so enter a dot in the Randy/Morse box. Don't forget, too, to enter X's in the boxes of the Morse column that correspond to the first names of the other boys.

Now that you know Randy is Morse, you are ready to look at what you've already discovered about Randy and transfer that information to the Morse column—remember that since Randy is Morse, anything that you know about Randy is also true of Morse, as they're the same person. You'll see that an X for Randy was entered from clue 3: Randy does not sell ice cream. Then Morse cannot be the ice cream seller either, so put an X in the Morse column to show that Morse doesn't sell ice cream.

Once the Morse/ice cream X is in place, note what you have established about the Wiley boy: His is the only last name left who can sell ice cream. Put the dot in the Wiley/ice cream box and enter X's in the Wiley column for all the other refreshments. Your next step? As before, you are ready to determine what this new dot will tell you, so you will go up to the other set of refreshment boxes and see what you have established about the ice cream vendor. He's not Noel or Steve—they have two X's already entered in the chart. Now that you have established the Wiley boy as the ice cream seller, you know that his first name can't be either Noel or Steve because neither of those boys sells ice cream. Once you've put X's in the Noel/Wiley box and the Steve/Wiley box, you'll see that you know who Wiley is. Remember that clue 4 had already told you that Andy's last name is not Wiley, so you have an X in the Andy/Wiley box. With the new X's, do you see that Wiley's first name has to be Chris? And since Chris is Wiley, and Wiley sells ice cream, so, of course, does Chris. Thus, you can put a dot in the Chris/ice cream box. And don't forget to put X's in the Chris row for the other refreshments and also in the ice cream column for the other first names.

Notice that once Chris Wiley is entered in the chart, there are now four X's in the Coble column, and Steve is the one who has to be the Coble boy. Put in the dot and then X's in the Steve row, and your chart looks like this:

	Coble	Davis	Morse	Smith	Wiley	candy	ice.	pean.	pop.	soda
Andy	X		X		X	X	X			
Chris	X	X	X	X	•	X	•	X	X	X
Noel	X		X	X	X		X			
Randy	X	X	•	X	X		X		X	
Steve	•	X	X	X	X		X	X		
candy	X	X			X					
ice.	X	X	X	X	•					
pean.		X			X					
pop.	X	•	X	X	X					
soda		X			X					

See that there are four X's in the Smith/first name column, so Smith's first name must be Andy. And Noel's last name is Davis, because he's the only one left. Remember—look down the Davis row and see—we already know Davis sells popcorn. So, Noel, whose last name is Davis, sells popcorn. And, of course, there should be X's in all the other boxes of the Noel row and the popcorn column.

Now that you have completely established two sets of facts—which first name goes with which last name—you can use the two sets of refreshment boxes almost as one. That is, since you know each boy's first name and last name, anything you have determined about a first name will hold true for that boy's last name; and, naturally, the reverse is true: whatever you know about a boy's last name must also be true of that boy's first name.

For example, you know that Coble is Steve, so look down the Coble column and note that you have already put X's in the candy, ice cream, and popcorn boxes. Go up to the Steve row and enter any X's that you know about Coble. After putting an X in the Steve/candy box, you'll see that you've determined that Steve sells soda. As always, don't forget to enter X's where appropriate once you've entered a dot to indicate a determined fact. These X's are what will narrow down the remaining possibilities.

Things are really moving fast now! Once you've entered the appropriate X's in the Steve row and the soda column, you will quickly see that there are four X's in the candy column—so, Randy (Morse) is the candy vendor. By elimination, Andy (Smith) sells peanuts and this Logic Problem is completely solved.

Many of the Logic Problems in this book will have charts that are set up much like the one in Example #2. They may be bigger, and the puzzle may involve matching more sets of facts, but the method of solving the Logic Problem using the chart will be exactly the same. Just remember:

Always read the whole problem through quickly. What you are to determine is usually stated in the last part of the introduction.

When using solving charts, use an X to indicate a definite impossibility and a • (dot) to indicate an established fact.

Once you have placed a dot to indicate an established fact, remember to put X's in the rest of the boxes in the row and the column that contains the dot.

Every time you establish a fact, it is a good idea to go back and reread the clues, keeping in mind the newly found information. Often, you will find that rereading the clues will help you if you seem to be "stuck." You may discover that you *do* know more facts than you thought you did.

Don't forget, when you establish a fact in one part of a solving chart, check to see if the new information is applicable to any other section of the solving chart—see if some X's or dots can be transferred from one section to another.

Just one other note before we get to Example #3, and this note applies to both the most inexperienced novice and the most experienced expert. If ever you find yourself stymied while solving a problem, don't get discouraged and give up—turn to the solution. Read the step-by-step elimination until you get to a fact that you have not established and see if you can follow the reasoning given. By going back and forth between the clue numbers cited in the solution and the clues themselves, you should be able to "get over the hump" and still have the satisfaction of completing the rest of the puzzle by yourself. Sometimes reading the solution of one puzzle will give you important clues (if you'll pardon the pun) to the thought processes involved with many other puzzles. And now to the last of our trio of examples.

Sometimes a Logic Problem has been created in such a way that the type of chart you learned about in Example #2 is not helpful in solving the problem. The puzzle itself is fine, but another kind of chart—a fill-in type—will better help you match up the facts and arrive at the correct solution. Example #3 is a puzzle using this type of solving chart.

EXAMPLE #3

It was her first visit home in ten years, and Louise wondered how she would manage to see her old friends and still take in the things she wanted to in the seven days she had to spend there. Her worry was needless, however, for when she got off the plane Sunday morning, there were her friends—Anna, Cora, Gert, Jane, Liz, and Mary—waiting to greet her with her seven-day visit all planned. The women knew that Louise wanted to revisit the restaurant where they always used to have lunch together, so Louise's vacation began that Sunday afternoon with a party. After that, each of the women had an entire day to spend with Louise, accompanying her to one of the following things: a ball game, concert, the theater, museum, zoo, and one day reserved for just shopping. From the clues below, find out who took Louise where and on what day.

1. Anna and the museum visitor and the woman whose day followed the zoo visitor were blondes; Gert and the concertgoer and the woman who spent Monday with Louise were brunettes. *(Note: All six women are mentioned in this clue.)*

2. Cora's day with Louise was not the visit that occurred the day immediately following Mary's day.

3. The six women visited with Louise in the following order: Jane was with Louise the day after the zoo visitor and four days before the museumgoer; Gert was with Louise the day after the theatergoer and the day before Mary.

4. Anna and the woman who took Louise shopping have the same color hair.

	Monday	Tuesday	Wednesday	Thursday	Friday	Saturday
friend						
activity						

As before (and always) read the entire puzzle through quickly. Note that here you are to determine which day, from Monday to Saturday, each woman spent with Louise and also what they did that day. The solving chart, often called a fill-in chart, is the best kind to use for this puzzle. You won't be entering X's and dots here; instead, you will be writing the facts into the chart as you determine them and also find out where they belong.

From clue 1 you can eliminate both Anna and Gert as the woman who took Louise to the museum and the concert. And neither of these activities took place on a Monday, nor did Anna or Gert spend Monday with Louise. You have discovered some things, but none of them can yet be entered into the chart. Most solvers find it useful to note these facts elsewhere, perhaps in the margin or on a piece of scratch paper, in their own particular kind of shorthand. Then when enough facts have been determined to begin writing them into the chart, you will already have them listed.

Do you see that clue 2 tells you Mary did not see Louise on Saturday? It's because the clue states that Cora's day was not the visit that occurred immediately following Mary's day, and thus, there had to be at least one visit after Mary's. You still don't have a definite fact to write into the chart. Don't lose heart, though, because . . .

. . . clue 3 will start to crack the puzzle! Note that this clue gives you the order of the six visits. Since the days were Monday through Saturday, the only possible way for Jane to be with Louise the day after the zoo visitor and four days before the museumgoer is if the zoo visit took place on Monday, Jane was with Louise on Tuesday, and the museumgoer was with Louise on Saturday. These facts can now be written into the chart—Monday zoo, Tuesday Jane, Saturday museum. Three days have been accounted for. The last part of clue 3 gives you the other three days: with Wednesday, Thursday, and Friday still open, the theatergoer must be the Wednesday friend, Gert is the day after, or Thursday, and Mary saw Louise on Friday. These facts, too, should be written in the chart. Once you've done so, your chart will resemble this one:

22

	Monday	Tuesday	Wednesday	Thursday	Friday	Saturday
friend		Jane		Gert	Mary	
activity	zoo		theater			museum

Now go back to clue 1 and see what other facts you can establish. There are three blondes—Anna, the museum visitor, and the woman whose day followed the zoo visitor's. The chart shows you that this last woman was Jane. From clue 4 you learn that the woman who took Louise shopping and Anna have the same color hair—blond. The woman who took Louise shopping is not Anna (they're two separate people), nor is she the museum visitor, so she must be the woman whose day followed the zoo visitor's, Jane. That fact can be written in the chart.

You can also, at this point, establish what day Anna spent with Louise. Since you know it's not Monday (clue 1) and Anna is not the museumgoer (also clue 1), the only day left for her is Wednesday, so Anna took Louise to the theater. Clue 2 tells you that Cora's day did not immediately follow Mary's, so Cora's day can't be Saturday, and must be Monday. By elimination, Liz (listed in the introduction) spent Saturday with Louise at the museum.

It may be helpful to make a note of the hair colors mentioned in clue 1, perhaps under the relevant columns in the chart. These hair colors can again be used at this point. We've now established the blondes as Anna, Jane, and Liz; the brunettes are Gert, the concertgoer, and Cora. The only possibility is that Mary is the concertgoer. Everything has now been determined except what Gert did, so, by elimination, Gert must have taken Louise to a ball game (from the introduction).

	Monday	Tuesday	Wednesday	Thursday	Friday	Saturday
friend	Cora	Jane	Anna	Gert	Mary	Liz
activity	zoo	shopping	theater	ball game	concert	museum
	bru	blo	blo	bru	bru	blo

Are all Logic Problems easy to solve? No, of course not. Many of the puzzles in this book are much more complicated than the three examples and should take a great deal more time and thought before you arrive at the solution. However, the techniques you use to solve the puzzles are essentially the same. All the information needed to solve will be given in the puzzle itself, either in the introduction or the clues. As you eliminate possibilities, you will narrow down the choices until, finally, you can establish a certainty. That certainty will usually help narrow down the possibilities in another set of facts. Once you have determined something, you will probably need to return to the clues and reread them, keeping in mind what facts you have now established. Suddenly a sentence in the clues may tell you something you could not have determined before, thus narrowing down the choices still further. Eventually you will have determined everything, and the Logic Problem will be solved.

EASY LOGIC PROBLEMS

1 LOGICAL FEAST

by Mary Marks Cezus

Carmela and three of her friends will be getting together Saturday night for a potluck supper. Each of the four, including Cook, will provide one item; one is making lasagna. Feed the clues below to your brain and see if you can determine each person's full name and what each will bring.

1. Frank is not the person who is bringing the green-bean casserole.

2. Ms. Bacon is on a diet and told Baker she would only be taking a tiny taste of his dish.

3. Taffy told the person preparing the tossed salad that she enjoys raw vegetables.

4. Both Sam and Rice think the woman who is bringing the tossed salad is much too thin and are glad she plans to eat freely of everything on Saturday night.

5. The person making the cheesecake asked Frank and Taffy which flavor they like best.

The solution is on page 139.

	Bacon	Baker	Cook	Rice	cheesecake	green-bean casserole	lasagna	salad
Carmela	X	X	X	●	X	X	X	●
Frank	X	●	X	X	X	X	●	X
Sam	X	X	●	X	●	X	X	X
Taffy	●	X	X	X	X	●	X	X
cheese-cake	X	X	●	X				
green-bean cass.	●	X	X	X				
lasagna	X	●	X	X				
salad	X	X	X	●				

27

2 BRAGGIN'

by Margaret Shoop

While four young boys were playing hard
Some rough-and-tumble game,
One bragged about how old he was;
So the others did the same.

We want to know how old each is,   5
And how old each claimed to be.
The facts that follow in this rhyme
Are enough, as you will see.

Each boy's really a different age,
In years they're seven to ten.   10
There were Johnny, Bill and dark-haired Max,
And Bill's only brother, Ben.

Blond Johnny claimed the age of eight,
The true age of another,
For Bill exclaimed, quite truthfully,   15
"That's the age of my brother."

Three overstated their ages,
And one gave just the facts;
And, we can tell you further, that
Bill's not as old as Max.   20

The years Max claimed, plus Ben's true years,
Add up to the number twenty.
Bill misstated his age by one year—
Now these are facts aplenty.

The solution is on page 139.

The REAL and CLAIM boxes have been left empty for you to fill in from the information found in the clues.

	REAL				CLAIM			
	7	8	9	10	8	10	8	12
Ben	✕	•	✕	✕	✝	✕	✝	
Bill	✕	✕	•	✕	✕	•	✕	
John	•	✕	✕	✕	•	✕	✝	✓
Max	✕	✕	✕	•	✕	✕	•	•

3 FAMILY NAMES

by W. H. Organ

The Joneses have named their four boys after favorite relatives; their friends, the Smiths, have done the same thing with their three boys. One of the families has twin boys. From the following clues, can you determine the full names of all seven children and their ages?

1. Valentine is four years older than his twin brothers.

2. Winston, who is 8, and Benedict are not brothers. They are each named after a grandfather.

3. Briscoe is two years younger than his brother Hamilton, but three years older than Dewey.

4. Decatur is 10 years old.

5. Benedict is three years younger than Valentine; they are not related.

6. The twins are named for uncles.

The solution is on page 139.

Use the charts below to fill in the information as you discover it from reading the clues. You will find these charts to be more helpful in solving this problem.

JONES

boy	age

SMITH

boy	age

4 APARTMENT PARKING

by Diane C. Baldwin

Ann, Frank, and two others rent the four apartments which are side by side on Grove Street and use the four reserved parking spaces, one in front of each apartment. From left to right the apartments are lettered A to D and the spaces are numbered 1 to 4. The four tenants each drive a different color (including green) and model car, one a station wagon. On a recent Saturday morning each tenant's car was parked in front of the apartments, though not necessarily in front of its owner's apartment. From the clues below, can you identify each tenant by full name, apartment letter, color and model of car, and parking location that particular morning?

1. The tenant in apartment C doesn't own the sedan.

2. The tenant in apartment A owns the car parked just to the right of the blue car and just to the left of the convertible, which isn't yellow.

3. The red car, which isn't the hatchback, is parked between Miller's and the sedan.

4. Both Don and Mr. White have end spaces but not end apartments.

5. Both tenant Logan's apartment and car are somewhere to the left of those of Jane's and those of Steele's.

The solution is on page 139.

We found this shortened version of the chart and the diagram of the apartments and parking spaces to be the most helpful.

	Logan	Miller	Steele	White	A	B	C	D	1	2	3	4
Ann												
Don												
Frank												
Jane												

	A	B	C	D
Apartments				
Parking spaces				
	1	2	3	4

5 PROM CHAPERONES

by Julie Spence

Last year, four teachers from Elwood high school and their spouses chaperoned the Senior Prom. From the clues below, can you determine the full name (one surname is Black) and occupation of each chaperone, and what subject each teacher teaches (one is an art teacher)?

1. Two of the chaperones were Chris and Carl.

2. These four are teachers: Mark, Theresa, Mr. Grey, and the math teacher.

3. One of the Whites is a pilot.

4. Bob is a salesman.

5. Amy is a secretary.

6. The English teacher's surname isn't Grey or Brown.

7. Rita, who isn't Mrs. Grey, is an attorney.

8. Matt's wife teaches science.

The solution is on page 140.

This fill-in chart was found to be the most helpful way of keeping track of the information found in the clues.

teacher	class	spouse	occupation	last name

6 STUFFED ANIMALS

by Claudia Strong

The McEvoys were recently on vacation and bought each of their four children (one of whom is Jessie) a stuffed animal as a souvenir. Hoping to avoid confusion and squabbles, they bought four animals which were clearly different types (one was a hippo) and different colors (one was yellow). Using the following clues, can you find each child's age (no two children are the same age and the ages are all one year apart, expressed in whole number of years) and the type and color animal each McEvoy child received?

1. Cyndi was so excited by her present, she ripped off the wrapping from her package first, followed by the three-year-old. Next the bunny was unwrapped and, finally, the blue toy was uncovered.

2. The eldest child (who was not Robin) received an orange animal as a gift.

3. Scott, who did not receive the raccoon, is a year younger than the child who received the lamb (which was not blue).

4. The two-year-old's toy was soon forgotten when a bright red toy was unwrapped immediately after it.

The solution is on page 140.

name	age	animal	color
Jessie			
Cyndi			
Scott			
Robin			

32

7 A ROUND OF GOLF

by Ellen K. Rodehorst

Jack and three other employees of the Pinecone Golf Course recently got together on their day off to play a round of eighteen holes of golf. Afterward, all four, including Green, went to the clubhouse to total their scorecards. Each man works at a different job (one is the short-order cook), and each shot a different score in the game. No one scored below 70 or above 85 strokes. From the clues below, can you discover each man's full name, job, and golf score?

1. Bill, who is not the maintenance man, plays golf often and had the lowest score of the foursome.

2. Clubb, who isn't Paul, hit several balls into the woods and scored ten strokes more than the pro-shop clerk.

3. Frank and the caddy scored, not necessarily respectively, four and seven strokes more than Sands scored.

4. Carter thought his score of 78 was one of his better games, even though Frank's score was lower.

5. None of the four scored 81 strokes.

handwritten notes:
clerk — pro-shop — x
Clubb — x+10
Sands — y
Frank — y+4(?)
caddy — y+4(?)
Carter 78
Frank <78
Sands Fr. Carter Clubb

The solution is on page 140.

It is up to you to determine the actual scores and fill them into the boxes in the chart.

	Bill	Frank	Jack	Paul	caddy	clerk	cook	maint. man	low		high 78 80
Carter	X	X	X	•					X	X	• X
Clubb	X	X	•	X		X			X	X	X •
Green	X	•	X	X					X	•	X X
Sands	•	X	X	X	X				•	X	X X
low		•	X	X	X	X		X			
high 78 80	78	• X	X X	X •	• X	X					
caddy	X	X									
clerk											
cook											
maint. man	X										

8 SPECIAL ARRIVALS

by Diane C. Baldwin

The Danielses and three other couples waited with growing excitement as their newly adopted babies were escorted off the plane from South Korea. As it happened, these particular families had all given the new arrivals new American first names, keeping the original Korean names as middle names. One baby had been given the name Joy and another David. One child's Korean name was Mee-sook. From the clues below, can you determine the full names of each adoptive couple (one wife is Linda and one husband is Bill) and the American and Korean names of their new child, as well as tell the order in which the children came off the plane?

1. The Clarks' daughter wasn't first off the plane, nor was the boy with the Korean name Chang-soo.

2. Jack and his wife and Dottie and her husband waited for their new sons, who did not exit consecutively.

3. The girl named Yung-hee in Korea was brought off just before the Potters' child and just after Tommy.

4. Jean's child, who isn't Molly, came off just after Jack's child.

5. Frank's daughter was escorted off sometime after Gail's daughter, but just before the child with the name Sung-chul.

6. The Doyles' child directly followed Harry's.

The solution is on page 141.

	Amer. name	Kor. name	father	mother	last name
1st					
2nd					
3rd					
4th					

9 ANImAL WELFARE

by Haydon Calhoun

A large housing development in Bright City has its own animal welfare center for the care and protection of neighborhood pets. One Saturday, Roy and four other youngsters either reported the loss of a pet, or found a stray and took it to the center to be claimed, or adopted a homeless cat or dog. Each animal was a different color—one of the five was black—and each child was involved in the welfare of only one particular animal. From the clues below, can you deduce the full name of each child (one surname is Pate) and tell whether he or she adopted, found, or lost a pet, and its kind and color?

1. The Kent child was not the one who lost a dog or the one who found a dog.

2. Vic lost his cat.

3. One youngster found a gray cat.

4. The dog that was adopted was not the white animal or the tan one.

5. Both Irene and the Otis child were involved with cats.

6. The Hall child, who is not Eve, was not involved with the spotted pet or with the adopted one, which are two different animals.

7. Joe, who was not involved with the tan pet, did not adopt an animal.

8. No one lost or found a white dog.

9. The Macy child was not the one who found a dog.

10. Neither the Kent child nor the Macy child adopted an animal.

The solution is on page 141.

	Hall	Kent	Macy	Otis	Pate
Eve					
Irene					
Joe					
Roy					
Vic					

first name	last name	found, lost or adopted	animal	color

10 FAVORITE PUZZLES

by Nancy R. Patterson

On the same day, three Dell subscribers from the East Coast of the United States and two, including Mike, from the West Coast, wrote to the editors asking for more of their favorite puzzles; one asked for more Anacrostics. From the clues below, can you figure out the full name of each subscriber (one surname is Cole) and which puzzle each prefers?

1. Neither Vic nor Jones is the Easterner who requested more diagramless crosswords.

2. Quinn and Smith are from the same coast.

3. Alma and Penny, who are both Easterners, have subscribed longer than the two who requested more Word Arithmetics and more Cross Sums, but not as long as Quinn.

4. Neither Alma nor Vic is Klein.

5. The two mathematical requests came from opposite coasts.

6. Jones isn't the one who likes Logic Problems.

7. Enid's request was for neither Word Arithmetic nor Logic Problems.

8. One man wrote from each coast.

The solution is on page 142.

The solution is on page 142.

	first name	last name	puzzle
West Coast			

East Coast			

36

11 A FRUITFUL EXPERIENCE

by Julie Spence

Staci and three other girls each prepared a fruit salad for a 4-H picnic. Each girl used three different kinds of fruit in her salad, and no two used the same combination of fruit. From the clues below, can you determine the full name of each girl (one surname is Jacobs) and the three kinds of fruit each used?

1. All the salads were made of some combination of apples, bananas, cherries and grapes.

2. Robin, who isn't the Miller girl, used apples.

3. The Clark girl used cherries and grapes, but the Flure girl only used one of these fruits.

4. Erica isn't the Miller or Clark girl.

5. Mandy and the Miller girl both used apples and cherries.

The solution is on page 142.

Keep in mind when filling in the chart that each girl used three different kinds of fruit.

	Clark	Flure	Jacobs	Miller	apples	bananas	cherries	grapes
Erica	X	X	●	X	X	●	●	●
Mandy	●	X	X	X	●	X	●	●
Robin	X	●	X	X	●	●	X	●
Staci	X	X	X	●	●	●	●	X
apples	●	●	X	●				
bananas	X	●	●	●				
cherries	●	X	●	●				
grapes	●	●	●	X				

12 THE FOUR FRIENDS

by Margaret Shoop

Four friends have always lived in the same town in four different residential areas: North Garden, South Garden, East Garden, and West Garden, which lie, respectively, due north, due south, due east, and due west of the town center. In driving to see one another, the four friends use the roads that run north-south and east-west through the town center. From the clues that follow, can you determine in which residential section each of the four lives now and where each lived prior to the move described in clue 1?

1. In June of last year, Betsy moved to the area where Terry was living and vice versa, with the result that Terry now lives farther north than Betsy.

2. Before Betsy and Terry moved last June, Dale drove straight ahead at the town center when visiting Betsy.

3. At present, Rob lives east of Dale and must turn left at the town center to visit Terry.

The solution is on page 142.

We found this map of the town to be more helpful than the usual solving chart.

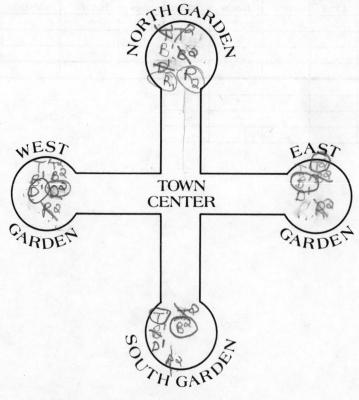

13 TWINS

Five sets of twins—including the Kirkmans—are in Miss Apple's first-grade class. Each set consists of a boy and a girl. The boys' names are Bobby, Gale, Gene, Jerry, and Lew. Oddly enough, the girls' names are Bobbie, Gail, Jean, Geri, and Lou. Only one brother and sister have the same sounding names. When speaking to them, Miss Apple also uses their middle names. From the clues below, can you determine each set of twins?

1. The Gardner girl and the Hampton boy have names that sound alike.

2. The Irving boy is neither Jerry nor Lew.

3. The five sets are: the Johnson twins, the Hampton twins, Gene and his sister, Bobby and his sister, and Bobbie and her brother.

4. Lou's last name is not Gardner.

5. Neither the Irving twins nor the Johnson twins is the set with the same sounding names.

The solution is on page 143.

	Bobby	Gale	Gene	Jerry	Lew	Gardner	Hampton	Irving	Johnson	Kirkman
Bobbie	X						X		X	
Gail										
Jean										
Geri										
Lou						X				
Gardner										
Hampton	X		X							
Irving				X	X					
Johnson	X		X							
Kirkman										

MEDIUM LOGIC PROBLEMS

14   QUICK CLEAN-UP

by Diane C. Baldwin

One Sunday afternoon Mr. and Mrs. MacNeil and their five children of different ages were relaxing in the living room when someone happened to look out the picture window and spot Great Aunt Melinda laboring up the hill to make a surprise visit. The place was a mess, with the Sunday paper and various other items strewn about the room. The whole family sprang into action, each child picking up one thing and quickly getting it out of sight while the parents rushed out to greet their guest. Each child chose a different hiding place, one behind a large pillow. From the clues below, can you tell who hid what and where, as well as the order of the children by age?

1. The child nearest Mack's age hid the snack dishes.

2. The five children are: Mandy, Mike, Matt (who are the three oldest, in some order), the child who hid the baseball glove, and the child who jammed something into the TV cabinet.

3. A girl stashed away the comic books while an older child pushed something under the sofa.

4. Neither the oldest nor the youngest—both boys—was the child who hid the toy cars, or the child who shoved something into the piano bench.

5. Mack didn't hide what was stuffed under the chair.

6. The child who hid what was pushed under the sofa was not Molly, Mike, or the child between them in age.

The solution is on page 143.

	chair	piano bench	pillow	sofa	T.V. cab.	base. glove	comic books	snack dishes	Sun. paper	toy cars	old-est			young-est
Mack	X	X	X	X	X	X	X	X	X	X	X	X	X	
Mandy	X		X	X	X	X	X	X	X	X			X	X
Matt	X	X	X	X	X	X	X	X		X	X	X	X	X
Mike		X	X	X	X	X	X	X	X	X	X	X	X	X
Molly	X	X	X	X		X	X		X	X	X	X	X	X

15 WORKING AT IT

by Cheryl L. McLaughlin

The McKays and four other couples living on Prosperity Drive are all two-income families; one of the ten is a dancer. From the following clues, can you determine the full names of each couple (one woman is Mary, and one man's first name is Simon) and all their occupations?

1. The five couples are Tara and her husband; the Lewises; the veterinarian and her husband; the broker and his wife, Liza; and John Callus and his wife, who isn't Dora or Kate.

2. Tony isn't the man who manages a hotel.

3. Earl's wife is a nurse.

4. The physician, a woman, is married to the lawyer.

5. The secretary, a man, isn't married to Kate, who is a designer; Dora, who isn't Mrs. Lewis, isn't Dave Collins' wife.

6. Mr. Davis, who is a bartender, isn't married to the veterinarian.

The solution is on page 143.

wife	occupation	husband	occupation	last name

16 SUNDAY BRUNCH

by Susan Zivich

Mr. and Mrs. Curtis hosted a Sunday brunch for their son and two daughters, and their spouses. The eight sat around a rectangular table, three on each side and one on each end. From the following clues, can you determine each person's full name (one first name is Steve) and where each sat? (*Note:* "Between" or "next to" can include around a corner of the table.)

1. As host, John Curtis sat at the head of the table.

2. Ellen noticed that each man sat between two women, and no one sat next to his or her spouse.

3. Mike is married to Nancy.

4. Jack sat between Tina and Mrs. Duncan.

5. Mary sat on her son's right.

6. The three people on each side of the table all had different last names. One of the last names was Bentley.

The solution is on page 144.

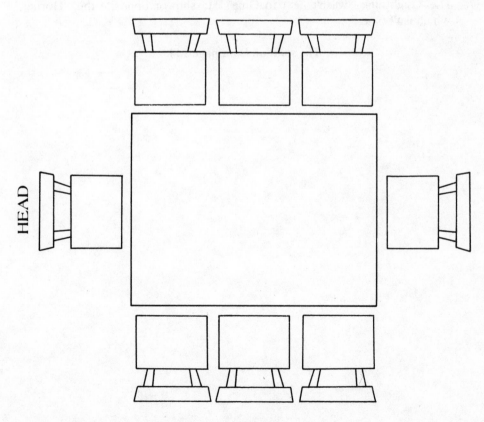

17 STARSHIP RIDE

by Diane C. Baldwin

Mark and five others rode solo but at the same time on the starship carnival ride. The ride had six different-colored starships (including green) attached in a circular fashion to evenly-spaced spokes which rotated clockwise as the starships glided forward and up and down. Every starship had a different name painted on its nose (including "Bullet"). From the clues below, can you determine the name and color of the starship each child rode, as well as its position in the circle?

1. Bob's starship flew directly behind a blue one and directly in front of the one named "Fireball."

2. The yellow starship wasn't behind Lisa's.

3. Boys and girls flew in alternate starships.

4. The "Blazer" was directly opposite Holly's and had a black starship and the "Hornet" on either side.

5. One of the girls flew in the "Comet," which isn't orange.

6. Dan, who didn't pilot either the "Blazer" or the red starship, had the orange starship next to him.

7. The "Lightning" wasn't next to Gina's starship or opposite the "Hornet," which isn't blue.

The solution is on page 144.

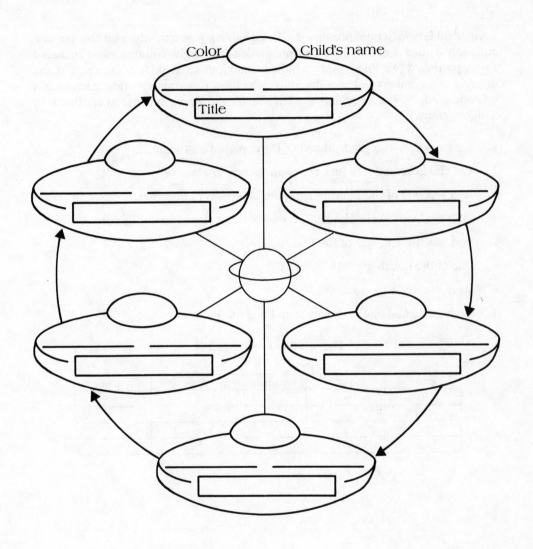

Color   Child's name

Title

18 THE THANKSGIVING PAGEANT

by Susan Zivich

Springfield Grade School presented a Thanksgiving pageant, with one boy and one girl representing each of the first four grades. The eight children, who included Ellen, portrayed two Pilgrims, two Indians, and four seasonal foods (one child was dressed as a cranberry). From the following clues, can you determine each child's role and grade? (*Note:* You may assume that a child who is older than another is in a higher grade.)

1. Karen, who was a grade ahead of Dave, played an Indian.

2. The child dressed as a turkey was in second grade.

3. Tina was one of the Pilgrims, and the other was her brother.

4. John and Anne were classmates; one of them played an ear of corn.

5. Bob was the younger of the two Indians.

6. One of the fourth-graders was a Pilgrim.

7. Steve dressed as a pumpkin.

8. Each grade had one people role and one food role.

The solution is on page 144.

grade	girl	costume	boy	costume
1st				
2nd				
3rd				
4th				

19 MOVING DAY

by Mary A. Powell

It was moving day in Zionsburg for five families, each of whom moved from one type of home to a different type of home. From the following clues, can you find the full name of each family member (one last name is Swanson), the type of home from which each moved, and the type of home each moved into? (*Note:* Married women have all assumed the surnames of their husbands, and only three types of homes are involved.)

1. When Robert was transferred from the city, he sold his condo to the Bentleys.

2. The widow who found her house too large for one person sold it to her newlywed daughter and son-in-law and moved into their rented apartment.

3. Sarah and her husband didn't moved from a rented apartment or to a rented apartment.

4. Steve and his wife didn't move from a house or to a house.

5. Neither Lois nor Karen has children and neither is the woman who is married to John.

6. David and his wife (who is not Karen) and the Madisons moved from rented apartments.

7. Mr. Fisher, who has never been married, moved into an apartment.

8. The Hunters helped Madeline move.

The solution is on page 145.

Mr.	Mrs.	last name	moved from	moved to

20 BOWLING TEAM DINNER

by Nancy R. Patterson

Last Wednesday evening, Dave and the other five members of his bowling team dined out together. Each man ordered either antipasto or minestrone to start with, and one of three entrees—lasagna, ravioli, or spaghetti. From the clues below, can you determine each bowler's full name (one surname is Noyes) and the two items he ordered?

1. Every order was different.

2. Bob, King, and a man who ordered ravioli all ordered one item in common; so did Chuck, Hall, and a man who ordered spaghetti. (*Note:* All six men are mentioned in this clue.)

3. Gary and White both ordered lasagna; Hall did not.

4. Frank didn't order minestrone; neither he nor Pinza ordered ravioli.

5. Neither Ed nor Frank is Veery.

The solution is on page 145.

first course	first name	last name	entree

21 THE PAINT WAS FREE

by Mary A. Powell

For the grand opening of their new paint department, Carpet Bazaar offered a free gallon of paint with each new carpet sold. Within the first hour of the sale, five couples bought new carpets. From the following clues, can you find the name of each couple, the color and style (tweed, solid, or patterned) carpet, and the color paint each chose? The colors available in both carpets and paints were: blue, brown, gold, green, and white.

1. No couple chose carpet or paint the same color as that described by their last name. No two couples chose the same color of paint or the same color of carpet.

2. The five couples are the Golds, the two who bought solid-color carpets, the one who bought the patterned carpet, and the one who chose gold paint.

3. The Greens and the couple who chose blue paint bought tweed carpets.

4. The Whites chose the same color paint as the Browns' carpet and the same color carpet as the Blacks' paint.

5. Two couples chose paint the same color as their carpets.

6. The green carpet was not a solid color.

The solution is on page 145.

last name	carpet		paint
	style	color	

51

22 FOOTBALL TICKETS

by W. R. Pinkston

Fred, a salesman, presented four of his best customers, including Bob, with two tickets each to Saturday's big football game and asked them to bring their wives. The eight tickets were all in a group consisting of seats J-116 through J-119 and seats K-116 through K-119 directly behind them. On Saturday, when Fred arrived at his own stadium seat directly across the field and aimed his binoculars at his customer's seats, he realized he had inadvertently mixed up the tickets: not one of his customers was seated next to his own wife. Just before the kickoff, Fred looked again and found that matters had been righted; seats had been exchanged and each couple were now seated side by side. From the following clues, can you determine the names of each couple (one wife is Beth), the original seating arrangement, and the arrangement after the exchange?

1. At first, seat J-116 was occupied by Gus; his wife was seated directly behind him.

2. Before the exchanges, Diane was in seat K-119, directly behind her husband.

3. In one exchange, Joe moved from Row K to Row J, trading seats with Ed.

4. The only other exchange involved Sandra's husband, who moved from Row J to Row K, trading seats with Mary's husband.

The solution is on page 146.

52

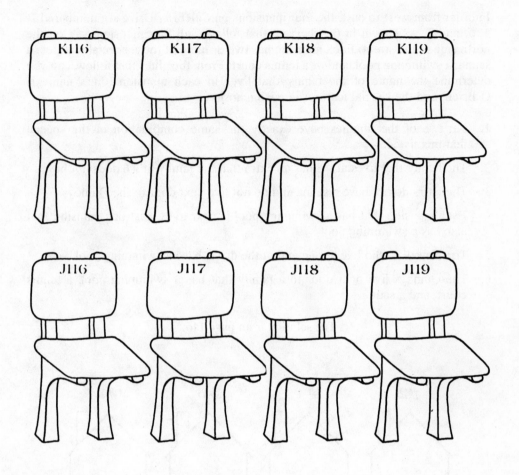

23 THE MANSIONS

by Margaret Shoop

In order from west to east, the four mansions on Celebrity Drive are numbered 2, 4, 6, and 8. As shown in the diagram that follows, all four mansions are on the north side of the street. Each mansion has two or more of these special features: a sauna, a swimming pool, and/or a tennis court. From the clues that follow, can you determine the name of the family that lives in each mansion (one's name is O'Brien) and the special features of each mansion?

1. No two of the families have exactly the same combination of the special features listed.

2. The family that lives at #8 has an extra that the family at #6 does not have.

3. The Parrs do not have a sauna and do not live next door to the Quincys.

4. Each mansion that has a swimming pool is next to at least one mansion that also has a swimming pool.

5. The Newells, who live at one end of the drive, have a swimming pool.

6. The Quincys live next door to a family that has a swimming pool, a tennis court, and a sauna.

The solution is on page 146.

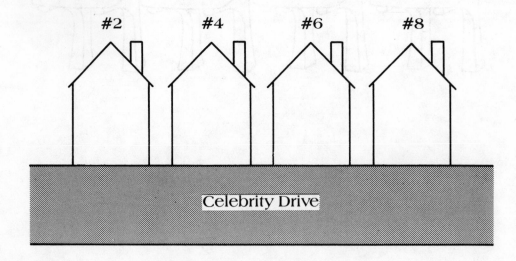

24 GRANDMA PERKINS' GIFTS

by W. H. Organ

The three Perkins children and the four Sweeney children are always sure of getting birthday cards from their grandmother Perkins, with brand-new, one-dollar bills enclosed—a dollar for each year of the child's age. Each family's children have birthdays in different months, but all seven birthdays occur in the last four months of the year, although all the children are different ages. From the following clues concerning last year's birthdays, can you determine the names of the children in each family, each child's birth month, and the amount each received?

1. Adele's brother Jon had his fourteenth birthday in September.

2. Candy's and Donald's birthdays are in October; Jane's and Elenita's are in November.

3. Ben, whose birthday is in September, found nine dollars in his card; one of his sisters found ten dollars in hers, the other sister, twelve.

4. Jane found thirteen dollars in her card.

5. One card contained eight dollars.

6. Donald received a bigger gift than Candy, but not as much as Jon.

The solution is on page 147.

month	name		amount
_____	_____	Perkins	_____
_____	_____	Perkins	_____
_____	_____	Perkins	_____
_____	_____	Sweeney	_____
_____	_____	Sweeney	_____
_____	_____	Sweeney	_____
_____	_____	Sweeney	_____

25 SPECIALTY CAMPS

by Evelyn Rosenthal

To help students with their summer plans, a school held a meeting at which several youngsters described their experiences the previous summer. The Unger girl and three others spoke about the specialty camps at which they had spent the summer, which were in four different states, including Michigan. From the following clues, can you find each girl's full name, her camp's specialty and state, and the order in which the girls spoke?

1. Audrey's camp is not the one in Ohio.

2. The Thomas girl spoke before the girl who spoke about her New York camp; the latter is not Carol.

3. Bess, who is not the Rogers girl, did not go to music camp.

4. Dora did not go to the Maine camp, which is not the one that specializes in sailing.

5. The girl who had gone to riding camp spoke right before Carol, who is not the Strong girl.

6. Audrey did not go to sailing camp.

7. The Rogers girl's camp is not in Ohio.

8. Audrey spoke before the girl who told about the tennis camp, who spoke right before the girl who had gone to camp in Maine.

The solution is on page 147.

	Rogers	Strong	Thomas	Unger	Me.	Mich.	N.Y.	Ohio	music	riding	sailing	tennis	1	2	3	4
Audrey					✕			✕	✕			✕				✕
Bess	✕								✕							
Carol		✕	✕				✕			✕			✕			
Dora					✕											
1			✕		✕		✕					✕				
2																
3																
4			✕							✕		✕				
music																
riding																
sailing					✕											
tennis					✕											
Me.																
Mich.																
N.Y.			✕													
Ohio	✕															

26 DEDICATED TO THE ONES I LOVE

by Julie Spence

Mystery author Blaze Chandler dedicated each of his first five novels, including *The Millstone Mystery,* to one of his five children. From the clues below, can you determine each child's name, current age (none are older than eighteen and all ages are in whole years), and the name of the novel dedicated to each?

1. *Private Puzzle* was dedicated to a girl who is half as old as her brother Van, who is half as old as his sister Ann.

2. Blaze dedicated *Fritz's Fantasy* to the child who is three years younger than his son Dan.

3. Blaze dedicated *Worried Willy* to a child who is younger than his daughter Jan.

4. Blaze's nine-year-old child is not the one to whom he dedicated *The Carlton Charade*.

5. *Fritz's Fantasy* was dedicated to a child nine years older than Nan, who is at least two years old.

The solution is on page 147.

age	name	novel

27 ANCESTRAL JOURNEYS

by W. H. Organ

It was a busy Monday for the Honolulu travel agent. She had prepared tickets for five local residents each with a different foreign destination, one of which was Tokyo. One of them was departing that same day, the others were each departing on different days until the following Sunday. Maria and the other four travelers all had "roots" in the countries they were visiting, all had at least one grandparent each who had come to Hawaii early in the century to work in the cane or pineapple fields and they hoped to learn something of their ancestors on their trips. From the following clues, can you determine each traveler's full name (one surname is Lee), occupation (one is a lawyer), destination, and day of departure?

1. George and Bryant were scheduled to leave on the weekend.

2. The nurse scheduled her departure one day earlier in the week than the traveler to Lisbon; neither flight was on the weekend.

3. The doctor's flight was earlier in the week than that of the traveler to Lisbon.

4. The writer's trip to Canton was not scheduled for Sunday.

5. Tim's destination was Dublin.

6. Carl, an engineer, scheduled his departure for Thursday.

7. Gary Young's destination was not Manila.

8. Jansen scheduled his trip later in the week than Burns, but he did not leave last.

The solution is on page 148.

TICKET ORDERS

Ticket 1

day _____

first
name _____

last
name _____

occ. _____

dest. _____

---

day _____

first
name _____

last
name _____

occ. _____

dest. _____

---

day _____

first
name _____

last
name _____

occ. _____

dest. _____

---

day _____

first
name _____

last
name _____

occ. _____

dest. _____

---

day _____

first
name _____

last
name _____

occ. _____

dest. _____

28 SWEET-TOOTH SATISFACTION

by Diane Yoko

When a box of candy was passed around at the end of a dinner party, Lynn and the other four guests each took one piece. Each piece was either dark or milk chocolate, and each had a different kind of filling; one was caramel. From the following clues, can you determine the full names of the five guests (one last name is Tyler), the kind of candy each chose, and the order in which the pieces were taken?

1. Only the first and last pieces of candy chosen were dark chocolate; the other three pieces were milk chocolate.

2. The candy with the mint filling was the fourth one chosen, followed by the piece Ms. Olson selected, which didn't have coconut filling.

3. The candy with vanilla filling was not the last piece taken.

4. Tara's candy was neither the one with coconut filling nor the one with mint filling.

5. The candy Larsen chose, which wasn't vanilla-filled, was taken immediately before Mary made her choice; Mary's candy was milk chocolate.

6. Tara took a piece of candy immediately after Davis, who took one immediately after the guest who chose the candy with chocolate filling, which wasn't the third piece taken.

7. Andy chose a piece of candy before Bill, who isn't Baker.

The solution is on page 148.

The solution is on page 148.

	1	2	3	4	5
first name					
last name					
filling					
dark or milk					

29 SHIPMATES

by Randall L. Whipkey

When they boarded the *Dick Tracy* for their second tours of duty, five ensigns who had been friends at the Shipping Academy found themselves together again after their first duty tours on different ships, one of which was the *Prince Valiant*. From the following clues, can you determine each officer's full name, the ship on which he served his first tour, and his assignment aboard the *Dick Tracy*?

1. At the Academy, Will, Ensign Stern, and the supply officer were all on the lacrosse team, while the man whose first tour of duty was on the *Steve Canyon* and Ensign Forward were both football players. (All five men are mentioned in this clue.)

2. While they were in school, Vic—who is not the munitions officer—was a company captain, while the man who served on the *Steve Roper*—who is not Ensign Bridges—was a squad leader.

3. Three men, Hugh, Ensign Briggs, and the recreation officer, all share one cabin, while the ensign who served on the *Phantom* and the communications officer share another.

4. Ensign Bulkhead is in charge of personnel.

5. Ted's last name is not Stern.

6. The supply officer, who is not Ensign Briggs, and the man who served on board the *Phantom* are both up for promotions.

7. Hugh did not serve on the *Charlie Brown*.

8. Stan and the ensign who served on the *Steve Roper,* who is not the communications officer, both plan on naval careers.

The solution is on page 148.

	Bridges	Briggs	Bulkhead	Forward	Stern	Com.	Mun.	Pers.	Rec.	Sup.	Canyon	C. Brown	Phantom	Roper	Valiant
Hugh															
Stan															
Ted															
Vic															
Will															
Canyon															
C. Brown															
Phantom															
Roper															
Valiant															
Com.															
Mun.															
Pers.															
Rec.															
Sup.															

30   I LOVE YOU

by Susan Zivich

One February 14th, Barbara sent a valentine to a favored boy, who sent his to another girl, who sent hers to another boy—and so on, until the eighth child sent a valentine to Barbara, completing the circle. From the clues below, can you determine each child's full name, the street on which each lives, and who received each child's valentine?

1. Though one boy and one girl live on each street, none of the children sent their valentines to someone on the same street.

2. Matt and the Walker child both live on Oak Street.

3. Roger sent his valentine to a child who lives on Maple Street, who sent hers to the Putnam child.

4. Jean and the Douglas boy live on Ash Street.

5. The Baxter boy sent a valentine to Pam.

6. Chuck and the Manning child both live on Maple Street.

7. Dave sent his valentine to the Clayborne child, who sent hers to a child from Oak Street.

8. Wendy and the Putnam child live on Elm Street.

9. The Johnson child sent a lacy valentine to the Rockwell child.

The solution is on page 149.

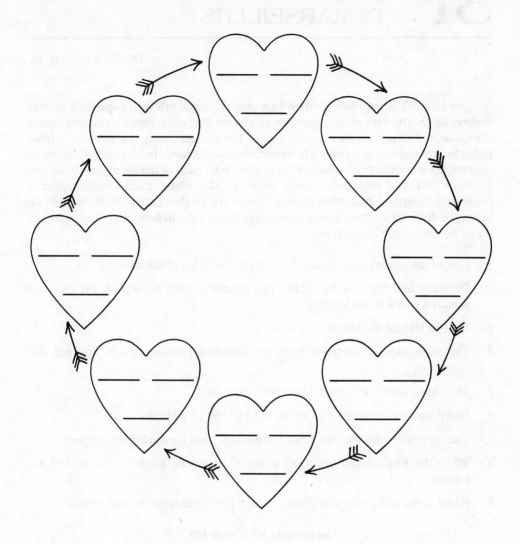

street   Boy   Girl

_____   _____   _____

_____   _____   _____

_____   _____   _____

_____   _____   _____

31 RENDEZVOUS IN MARSEILLES

by W. H. Organ

Jacques Benoit's latest novel deals with an international effort to cope with certain lawless elements. His chief character is named Pierre, a French security agent stationed in Paris, who meets with five of his foreign counterparts (one is from Italy) to exchange information. The rendezvous takes place in Marseilles. To better conceal his movements en route to the rendezvous, each of the six agents used two different means of transportation to arrive in Marseilles. Each choose either a plane or a train and one other form of travel which differed from all the others. From the following clues, can you determine each agent's country and mode of travel for each leg of his journey?

1. One of the agents used a bicycle on the second leg of his journey.

2. Donald's first leg was by plane; the Spaniard rode horseback for the first hundred miles of his journey.

3. Horace started his journey by bus.

4. The agent who started by train and finished by motorcycle was not the American.

5. The Greek agent arrived in Marseilles by train.

6. Philip was the only agent to arrive in Marseilles by plane.

7. The bicyclist, who was not Carl, traveled by train for part of his journey.

8. When the Englishman deplaned in Paris, he rented a car for the rest of his journey.

9. Raoul traveled by ship and plane, though not necessarily in that order.

The solution is on page 149.

agent's country	agent's name	first leg	second leg

64

32 WORD POWER

by W. R. Pinkston

An elementary-school teacher read a report on the results of a test given to a group of college students to determine the extent of their vocabularies, and she was surprised at the large list of words that none of the students recognized. Later, she asked five of her best sixth- and seventh-grade pupils if they could define any of the five words she put on the blackboard (one word was *quidnunc*). While the pupils could not even guess the meanings of most of the words, each of the five "defined" (incorrectly) one word (one offered "grouch" as a definition). Oddly enough, each student "defined" a different word. From the following clues, can you find each pupil's name and grade, the word each attempted to define, and the "definition" each furnished?

1. The child who attempted to define *dichotomy* was not a sixth-grade girl; the one who offered "sermon" as a definition was not a sixth-grade boy.

2. A seventh-grade girl, who wasn't Beth, offered "English coin" as a definition; she didn't define *dichotomy*, nor was she the child who attempted to define *widgeon*.

3. A sixth-grade boy, who wasn't Bob, offered a definition of *gerbera;* he wasn't the child whose definition was "gadget."

4. Neither Lucy nor Eva was the child who tried to define *eidolon*.

5. Ray and Eva are in the same grade.

6. The boy who gave "sermon" as a definition wasn't the child who attempted to define *eidolon*.

7. "Medicine" was offered as a definition by a seventh-grader.

8. One of the five pupils is a seventh-grade boy.

The solution is on page 150.

grade	name	word	"definition"

65

33 GLADYS GROWS GLADS

by Julie Spence

Gladys Gladstone, who lives at 202 Flower Lane, has a flower garden and grows only one kind of flower, gladiolas. One day while walking along her street, Gladys noticed that each of her neighbors grows a flower that could be a woman's name, but that no woman, except Gladys, grows a flower which reflects her own name. Gladys's neighbors live in adjacent houses on the same side of the block (numbers 204, 206, 208, 210, and 212), and each grows only one kind of flower (one grows dahlias). From the information below, can you determine each neighbor's full name, flower, and address?

1. The woman who grows daisies lives at a lower house number than Lily, and at a higher number than Ms. Brown.

2. Daisy lives next door to the woman who grows roses.

3. Ms. Black, who is not Rose and is not at the highest house number, does not live next door to Gladys or Lily.

4. The woman who grows lilies lives at number 208.

5. Ms. Gray lives at a higher number than Ms. White, who does not live next door to the woman who grows violets.

6. Ms. Green does not grow daisies, nor does she live next door to the woman who does.

7. Neither Dahlia's nor Violet's surname is Black.

8. No woman grows flowers reflecting the name of her next-door neighbor.

The solution is on page 150.

34 THE EXPLORERS QUIZ

by Evelyn Rosenthal

On an unexpected quiz, the fourth-grade class was given a list of five Spanish explorers and a list of five discoveries and asked to match them; most did so correctly, pairing Balboa and the Pacific, Cortez and Mexico, De Leon and Florida, De Soto and the Mississippi, and Pizarro and Peru. Three children, however, had not studied the lesson and failed miserably. From the following clues about those three, can you find the discovery each attributed to each explorer?

1. Each of the three had one and only one correct answer.

2. One discovery was attributed by John to De Soto, by Andy to Balboa, and by Sally to De Leon; all three were wrong.

3. No two of the three children agreed on any of the five answers.

4. The same explorer was called the discoverer of Peru by Sally, of the Pacific by John, and of the Mississippi by Andy; all three were wrong.

5. One of the three correctly identified De Soto's discovery, and one knew—or guessed—the right explorer of Peru.

The solution is on page 150.

correct answers	Andy	John	Sally
Balboa-Pacific			
Cortez-Mexico			
De Leon-Florida			
De Soto-Mississippi			
Pizarro-Peru			

35 THE SCHOONER'S CREW

by W. H. Organ

Pierre Barbot, owner and skipper of the schooner *TradeWind,* is well satisfied with the crew he has gathered together while operating in the South China Sea. It was just four years ago that he hired the first man, and at varying intervals since that time, he signed up the other five. Each man was hired in a different port; one port was Davao. Each can speak only one language, and all the tongues are different (one is Spanish); however this poses no problem, as all of them are fluent in the use of pidgin, that universal tongue of the waterfront in the Orient. From the following clues, can you determine the name of the port in which each man was hired, the language he speaks, and the time he has served on the *TradeWind*? (Note: Do not assume that the language spoken by a crew member is necessarily that of the country in which his sign-on port is located.)

1. The crew member who signed on at Macao has served a year less than Dirk and six months longer than the crew member who joined the ship at Manila, who is not the one who speaks Moro.

2. The crew member who signed on at Singapore speaks Portuguese; he is not Kriss.

3. Joe, who speaks Malay, has served for just one year, the shortest period.

4. Kim, the third to be hired, has served a year more than Shark.

5. The crew member who was hired in Hong Kong has served twice as long as Kriss and four times as long as the crew member who joined at Saigon.

6. Lum, who speaks Chinese, was not the first to be hired.

7. One of the crew members has served eighteen months.

8. Dirk is not the one who speaks Tagalog, nor does he speak Moro.

The solution is on page 151.

order hired	length of service	name	port	language
1				
2				
3				
4				
5				
6				

36 EIGHT KIDS AND ONE BATH

by Margaret Shoop

With eight children and just one bath, the Morgans have found it necessary to get up very early themselves to use the bath between 5:30 and 6:00 and to designate a scheduled amount of time for each child after that. The schedule allows each boy ten minutes and each girl fifteen minutes, with the first child scheduled to begin at 6 A.M. Although the schedule usually isn't followed to a tee, it does serve as a guideline which makes it possible for the children to catch their school buses when they arrive. From the clues that follow, can you deduce each child's scheduled bathroom-use time and age (the ages range from 6 to 12 years, with no two being the same age except for the one set of twins)?

1. Bill, who isn't a twin, and Darryl are a year apart in age, and Darryl is a year older than Christopher.

2. Christopher is supposed to be finished in the bathroom at 7 A.M.

3. The first to use the bathroom is a girl; the next to use it is supposed to begin on the same minute that she finishes.

4. Jim, who is 12, uses the bath later than Michelle, who uses it just after Darryl.

5. The child who is scheduled to begin use of the bathroom at 6:35 is 8 years old.

6. Holly is 11 years old.

7. Lois is a year younger than Kate; Lois uses the bathroom just before Kate.

8. The two who are twins use the bath one after the other.

9. The child who uses the bath right after Jim is 6 years old.

The solution is on page 151.

The solution is on page 151.

time	name	age
6:00–		

age	name
6	
7	
8	
9	
10	
11	
12	

37 THE RECITAL

by Haydon Calhoun

For their senior recital at Bonneville Conservatory, Upton and seven other music students performed W.A. Schmaltz's *Four Seasons,* a composition of four different duets for piano and violin. Each pair of musicians, one was Joyce, in turn played a different duet; one was entitled "Autumn." From the clues below, can you determine the order in which the four duets were played, and the full names and instruments of the players who performed each?

1. Young, who isn't a pianist and didn't perform first, played immediately before "Summer" was performed.

2. Ralph performed immediately before pianist Dills, who played immediately before "Winter" was performed.

3. Nancy performed before Dills, who played immediately before Hiram.

4. Karen performed before Quest, who didn't perform last.

5. Melba performed before at least two other duos.

6. Oscar, whose last name isn't Quest, didn't play "Summer."

7. Early performed neither first nor last.

8. Dills, whose first name isn't Melba, didn't play "Summer."

9. Inman, who isn't Tommy or a violinist, didn't perform first.

10. Levin isn't Nancy or Ralph.

11. Grant isn't Ralph or a pianist and didn't play "Spring."

The solution is on page 152.

The solution is on page 152.

title	piano		violin	
	first name	last name	first name	last name

38 SUPER ATHLETES

by Margaret Shoop

Ms. Pauley and four other girls recently vied in the finals of a contest to find their school's "super athlete of girls." The finals consisted of competition in four events: 200-meter freestyle swimming, 55-yard dash, modified pushups, and basketball goal shooting. Five points were awarded for winning an event, 4 points for coming in second, and so forth, with one point being given for coming in last. Each girl's total score was the sum of her scores in the four events. Some of the results of the competition are shown in the chart that follows. From the chart entries and the clues that are given, can you complete the chart, thus determining the order of finish for the contest?

1. Marcie didn't finish last in the pushups event.

2. Jane and Ms. Finney got the same total score.

3. Ms. Dunn isn't the girl who got two second-place finishes.

4. Liz got the same score in two events.

5. Ms. Newton scored two places higher than Marcie in the pushups event.

6. Elena had no fourth-place finishes.

7. Ms. Moore's points for the 55-yard dash exactly equaled Kathleen's for the 200-yard freestyle event.

The solution is on page 152.

First Name	Last Name	200-meter freestyle	55-yard dash	Pushups	Basketball throw	TOTAL
	Dunn	5				
Marcie			3			
	Moore	3		5		
			1		2	9
Liz				3	1	10
TOTAL		15	15	15	15	60

39 TUG OF WAR

by Cheryl L. McLaughlin

At an annual company picnic, Rob and seven others participated in a tug-of-war contest, with four people on each team; the eight included the company president. The two teams were ranged along the rope as shown to the right. From the following clues, can you determine the full name (one surname is Young) and position of each person along the rope?

1. The personnel and sales managers were on the same team as Cathy and Fox; the sales manager was on the same team as, and directly behind, Mr. Lentz.

2. There were at least three people between Brown and Tom, who was to Brown's left. (*Note:* "Left" means as viewed by you, the solver.)

3. Bea, who is the vice president, and Pam were on opposite teams.

4. Sara (who isn't Smith) and Dave (who isn't the sales manager) were at opposite ends of the rope; Sara was directly behind Mr. Werr, the accountant.

5. Al was directly to the left of the treasurer, who was not on his team.

6. Cane was on the same team as the file clerk; Mr. Jones, who isn't the secretary, was on the opposing team.

The solution is on page 153.

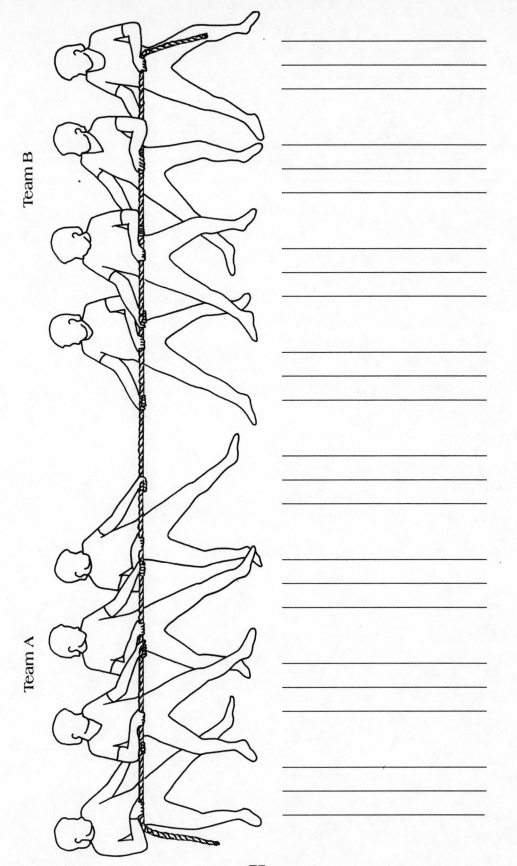

75

HARD LOGIC PROBLEMS

40 TELEPHONE TIE-UP

by Diane C. Baldwin

One night while he was away on a business trip, Mr. Doyle tried repeatedly to call home, starting at eight o'clock, but the phone was continuously busy until nine, when he finally got through. It turned out that Holly, Joe, and his two other teenage children had each called a friend. The first call had been made at eight, and no sooner had one youngster hung up than another picked up the phone to make an "absolutely necessary" call; one had to discuss an upcoming party. All the calls were different lengths, and each lasted a multiple of five minutes. From the following clues, can you figure out who called whom (one of those called was a girl named Patty), and the length of each call?

1. A girl called Rick; theirs was not the conversation about the basketball game.

2. The call to Brian took half as long as the one Tom made.

3. Cathy wasn't one of the two girls who discussed the French homework.

4. Two boys had the shortest conversation; neither they nor the ones who talked the longest were the pair who discussed movies.

5. Karen's call took twice as long as the one about French.

The solution is on page 153.

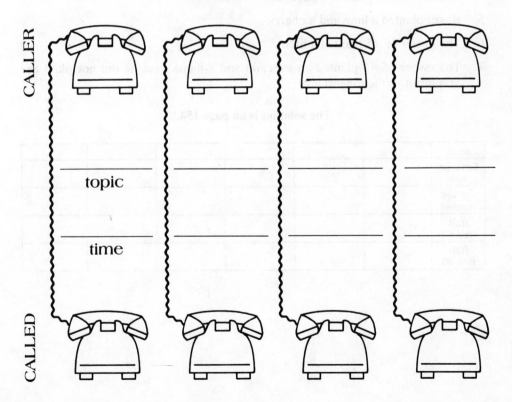

41 ALOHA GARDENS

by W. H. Organ

Aloha Gardens is a small condominium complex consisting of six cottages in a garden-like setting. The cottages are spaced around a swimming pool and are numbered from #1 to #6 in no particular order. Shortly after the cottages were built, each owner (one is named Saunders) planted two fruit trees and one flowering tree adjacent to his residence. None of the twelve fruit trees were the same (one was a mango), and the flowering tree which each owner planted was either a plumeria or a flame tree, neither of which bore fruit. Five of the fruit trees were citrus—orange, lemon, lime, tangerine, and grapefruit—each planted by a different owner. From the following clues, can you determine each owner's cottage number and the trees he planted?

1. Cooper and the owner of #4 cottage planted flame trees; neither planted an orange tree.

2. Hubbard planted a plumeria; one of his fruit trees was a pomegranate, the other was not a papaya.

3. Two of Barnes' trees were a plumeria and a banana. His neighbor in #2 planted a flame tree and an orange.

4. One of Nelson's trees was a plumeria; he did not plant the grapefruit. His neighbor in #3 planted a papaya.

5. Baker planted a lime and a cherry.

6. The owner of #5 planted a litchi.

7. The owner of #1 planted an avocado and a flame tree; he did not plant the grapefruit or the tangerine.

The solution is on page 154.

The solution is on page 154.

name						
flowering tree						
cottage number						
fruit tree #1						
fruit tree #2						

42 GIFT SUBSCRIPTIONS

by W. R. Pinkston

George, who has been considering reading more periodicals, was recently surprised to receive five notices of birthday gift subscriptions, including one to a magazine called *Aspect;* at least one of the five publications is a monthly. George calculates that the gifts will increase his receipt of magazines in the mail by one hundred over the next year. From the following clues, can you determine each magazine's subject matter (one is business) and frequency of publication, as well as the family member who gave George each subscription?

1. Neither *Jornada* nor *Quinta* is the literary journal or the science magazine; both of the former were gifts from women.

2. The weekly, which isn't the travel magazine, and the one called *Stratum* were both gifts from men.

3. George's niece's gift furnishes more annual copies than either his son's gift or his sister's.

4. The science magazine isn't the quarterly.

5. The gardening magazine is published more often than the science magazine but less frequently than the literary journal, which isn't the weekly.

6. *Quinta* is published more often than the gift from George's daughter.

7. *Epitome* wasn't George's cousin's gift.

8. One of the magazines is published bimonthly.

The solution is on page 154.

	business	gardening	literary	science	travel	frequency				son	daughter	niece	sister	cousin
Aspect														
Epitome														
Jornada														
Quinta														
Stratum														
son														
daughter														
niece														
sister														
cousin														
frequency														

43 WEDDING BELLS

by Susan Zivich

Five couples, all consisting of brothers and sisters from five different families, decided to get married in one huge ceremony. Mr. Nelson and his sister were among the brides and grooms on this auspicious day. There was one sister and one brother from each family. One bride was Ellen, and one of the grooms was David. From the following clues, can you determine who married whom and in what order the five couples exchanged vows? (*Note:* All five brides adopted their husbands' surnames.)

1. Karen and her groom exchanged vows just after her brother and his bride.

2. Jean's new surname is Williams.

3. Allan and his bride were the first to exchange vows.

4. The second couple to exchange vows were a Williams and an Andrews.

5. John married Mary, who is not Edward's sister.

6. Miss Banks and her groom were the third couple to exchange vows.

7. Nancy and her groom, who were not the last to exchange vows, did so right after Miss Miller and her groom.

8. The last couple to exchange vows included neither Mary Andrews nor Mr. Banks.

9. Peter's last name is Miller.

The solution is on page 155.

| | groom | | bride | |
	first name	last name	first name	last name
first				
second				
third				
fourth				
fifth				

44 JOBS AND HOBBIES

by Harry Faske

Six men hold six different jobs, and pursue six different hobbies—each of the latter, as it happens, akin to the occupation of one of the others. One, for example, is a forest ranger, while another spends his weekends camping; one is a TV repairman, another an electronics hobbyist; one is a cab driver and another races cars for fun. Two of the six make jewelry. From the following clues, can you determine each man's job and hobby?

1. Al's hobby is Ed's occupation.
2. Barney and Ed are photographers.
3. One of the drivers is a carpenter.
4. Charlie and Dick are the outdoorsmen.
5. Frank is a carpenter.
6. Charlie's occupation, which is not cab driving, is Frank's hobby.
7. Al's occupation is Dick's hobby.
8. The forest ranger does not make jewelry.

The solution is on page 155.

name	occupation	hobby

45 TRUCKERS' LOADS

by Diane Yoko

Each of the five truck drivers, including one who lives in North Dakota, left his or her home state with a load, hauled it to another state where the rig was reloaded, and then returned home with the second load. From the following clues, can you determine the state where each one lives, the first and second loads each hauled—one load was fabricated metal—and the state of his or her first delivery (one driver reloaded in Florida)?

1. Both the driver from New Mexico and a woman who reloaded in Oklahoma own their rigs; John, whose first load was books, and the one from Indiana both drive company trucks.

2. The driver from New York didn't haul potatoes on either trip.

3. The woman from Pennsylvania left her state with leather.

4. Neither leather nor peanuts was delivered to Oklahoma.

5. The lumber wasn't exchanged for paper.

6. Neither the woman who went to Wisconsin nor the person whose first load was electronic equipment reloaded with tires.

7. The rig driven to Wyoming is owned by its driver.

8. Wayne didn't haul tires.

9. Rich isn't the driver from New Mexico, nor is he the one whose first load was lumber.

10. Lynn didn't haul cord or paper, nor was paper the merchandise reloaded in Iowa.

11. Betty hauled only edibles.

The solution is on page 156.

	home state					reloaded					cargo out					cargo back			
	Ind.	N.D.	N.M.	N.Y.	Pa.	Fla.	Iowa	Ok.	Wis.	Wyo.	books	elec. eq.	leather	lumber					
Betty																			
John																			
Lynn																			
Rich																			
Wayne																			
cargo back																			
cargo out	books																		
	elec. eq.																		
	leather																		
	lumber																		
reloaded	Fla.																		
	Iowa																		
	Ok.																		
	Wis.																		
	Wyo.																		

46 NECKLACE PENDANTS

by Claudia Strong

Lea is a jewelry artist who, last week, made 25 necklace pendants to sell in her crafts store. Each was made of glass, metal, or ceramic; was orange, red, or yellow in color; and was in the shape of a star, sunburst, or crescent moon. From the following information, can you find the types of pendants and the number(s) of each that Lea made last week?

1. A total of twelve pendants were yellow, and a total of eleven were made of glass; a total of six were made of yellow glass.

2. Lea made only two orange sunbursts last week, both of the same material.

3. All the glass pendants which were not yellow were either stars or sunbursts, and exactly half of the star-shaped ones in this group were orange.

4. Of the yellow pendants which were not sunbursts, there was one more star than moon, and all the yellow moons were made of metal.

5. Lea made a total of eight sunburst pendants; of these, five were yellow and three were glass, but only two were yellow glass.

6. The pendants that were not yellow, made of glass, or shaped like sunbursts were equally divided among orange ceramic moons, orange ceramic stars, and red metallic stars.

7. No sunburst was made of metal.

The solution is on page 156.

	stars			sunbursts			moons		
	O	R	Y	O	R	Y	O	R	Y
glass									
metal									
ceramic									

47 THE EXERCISE REGIMEN

by Margaret Shoop

Lee and four of her friends have just completed an exercise regimen designed to improve their physical fitness and reduce their weight. Their heights are different whole numbers of inches and range from 5′2″ to 5′6.″ The last name of one of the five is Strasberg. With the information already in the chart and the following clues, can you fill in the missing data?

1. Each of the five has lost a whole number of pounds, none more than twenty-five; no two have lost the same amount.

2. Gomez is 5′2″ tall.

3. One of the five weighed 120 pounds before starting the regimen.

4. The woman who is 5′4″ tall weighed the same as one of the other four before the regimen was begun; now, she weighs fifteen pounds less than that woman.

5. Gold has lost twice as much as Gladys.

6. Gold is the tallest of the five, and she and Erica now weigh the same.

The solution is on page 156.

first name	last name	height	original weight	new weight	pounds lost
Mary					15
	Brown		140		
	Richards				10
Phyllis				125	
		5′3″			5

87

48 MOSQUITO PASS

by Nancy R. Patterson

In an all-day race for harnessed pairs of burros, Mr. Sutton and four other owners led their teams across Mosquito Pass at speeds approaching three miles an hour. Not necessarily in order of finish, the "near" burros (those hitched on the left) were Brazen, Bronx, Conviction, Monument, and Shane. Not necessarily respectively, their "off" partners (those hitched on the right) were Ears, Hotee, Mistake, Queens, and Tripod. From the following clues, can you match up the teams, identify their owners by full name, and specify the order of finish?

1. The five burro owners are Duke, Mr. Easton, the two men who own Brazen and Mistake, and the man whose team came in first.

2. Bronx and Queens were paired; they finished immediately ahead of Mr. Norton's team and immediately behind Zeke's.

3. Tripod beat both Mr. Weston's team and the team that included Hotee (which was not paired with Brazen).

4. Monument wasn't part of the fourth-place team.

5. Mr. Easton's team finished ahead of Conviction and immediately behind Abner's team, which included Ears.

6. Jake doesn't own Conviction or Tripod.

7. Ike isn't Mr. Weston or Mr. Upton.

The solution is on page 157.

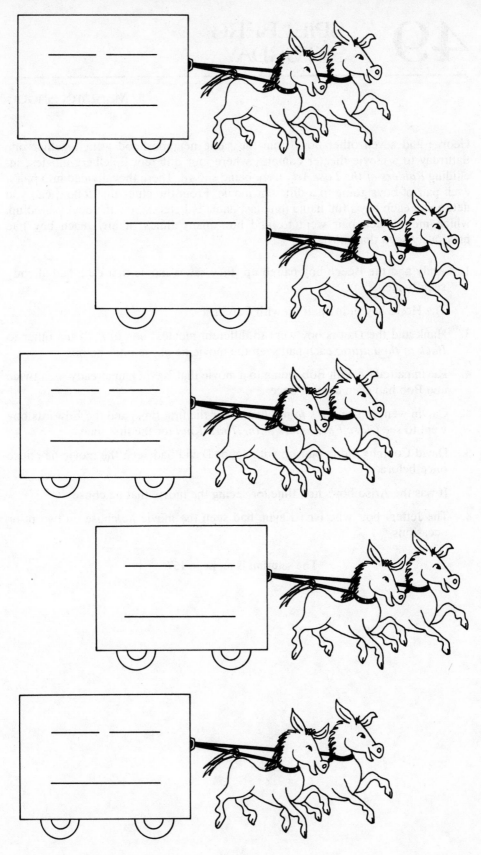

89

49 SPIELBERG SATURDAY

by Margaret Shoop

George and seven other boys from the same neighborhood went together one Saturday to a movie-theater complex where four different Spielberg movies, including *Raiders of the Lost Ark,* were being shown. There they divided into pairs, each pair of boys going to a different movie. From the clues that follow, can you determine each boy's full name (one last name is Peters), how the boys paired up, which movie each pair went to, and how many times (if any) each boy had previously seen that movie?

1. Andy and the Beech boy paired up; they saw a movie that each had already seen twice.

2. The Howe boy didn't pair up with Calvin.

3. Hank and the Dawes boy went to different movies, one to *E.T.,* the other to *Back to the Future;* each had seen the movie he chose once before.

4. Kevin paired up with Bob, going to a movie that Kevin had already seen twice and Bob had seen at least once.

5. Calvin went to see *Back to the Future* for the first time, and the Edwards boy went to see *Close Encounters of the Third Kind* for the first time.

6. David Coombs didn't pair up with John; David had seen the movie he chose once before.

7. It was the Ariso boy's first time for seeing the movie that he chose.

8. The Jeffers boy, who isn't Kevin, had seen the movie he chose on two prior occasions.

The solution is on page 157.

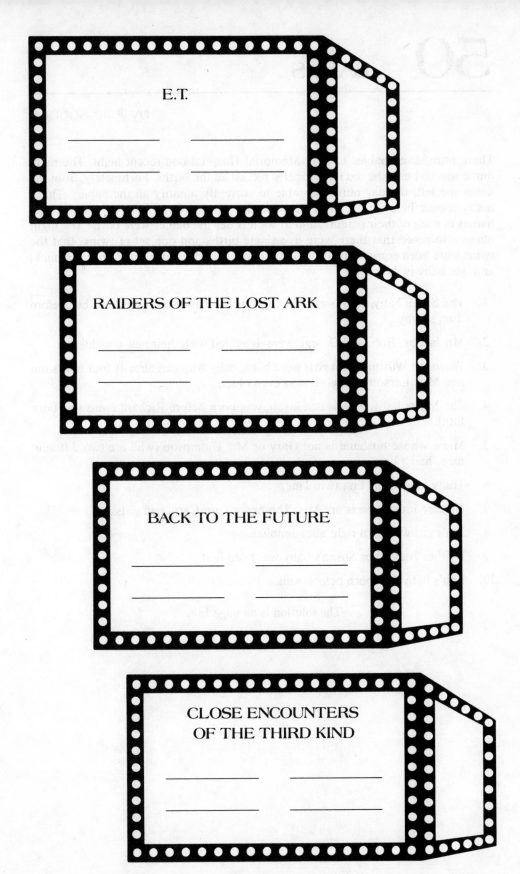

E.T.

_____   _____

RAIDERS OF THE LOST ARK

_____   _____

_____   _____

BACK TO THE FUTURE

_____   _____

_____   _____

CLOSE ENCOUNTERS
OF THE THIRD KIND

_____   _____

_____   _____

91

50 BABES

by Julie Spence

There were seven babies born at Memorial Hospital one recent night. The night nurse was so busy she did not properly record all the births. Fortunately, from the notes she left, the day nurse was able to correctly identify all the babies. Those notes appear below. Can you determine the names of the babies born, the full names of each of their parents, and in what order the babies were born? The night nurse also noted that there were five single births and one set of twins, that the twins were born consecutively, and that one mother is Betty, one father is Chuck, and one baby is Amy.

1. The Smith baby, who is not Gary's, was born after baby Andrew, but before Tom's baby.

2. Mr. Jacobs, Bob, and George were delighted with their new daughters.

3. When the Wilsons' twin girls were born, baby Ann was already four hours old and Mrs. Larson's daughter was even older.

4. The Miller baby, who is not Jason, was born before Richard (who was born fifth).

5. Mary, whose husband is not Gary or Mr. Thompson (who are two different men) had a boy.

6. Trudy named the first twin Jane.

7. Neither Judy (who is not Mrs. Thompson) nor Carol had girls.

8. Jim's girl was born right after Jennifer.

9. Neither Judy's nor Susan's baby was born first.

10. Bob's baby was born before Ann.

The solution is on page 158.

1. BABY

MOM_____

DAD_____

_____

2. BABY

MOM_____

DAD_____

_____

3. BABY

MOM_____

DAD_____

_____

4. BABY

MOM_____

DAD_____

_____

5. BABY

MOM_____

DAD_____

_____

6. BABY

MOM_____

DAD_____

_____

7. BABY

MOM_____

DAD_____

_____

51 AIRLINE COUNTER

by Nancy R. Patterson

One recent afternoon, Bob, Lois, and three others stood in line for tickets at an airline counter; one of the five was bound for Chicago. From the following clues, can you deduce each traveler's full name (one surname is Girard) and destination, and the order in which the five waited in line?

1. Although not last in line, the passenger for St. Paul stood farther back than either Dawes or the passenger for Seattle (which wasn't Jean's destination).

2. Tom stood farther back than Elkins, but he wasn't last in line.

3. Alice stood just in front of Mr. Foley and just behind the passenger for Atlanta.

4. Although not first in line, the passenger for Dallas stood just ahead of Hall; neither of these two is Tom.

5. Alice's last name isn't Elkins.

The solution is on page 158.

The solution is on page 158.

	first name	last name	destination
1	_____	_____	_____
2	_____	_____	_____
3	_____	_____	_____
4	_____	_____	_____
5	_____	_____	_____

by Randall L. Whipkey

Among the items offered in the Summerset Charity Auction were five pottery toby mugs, each depicting a famous historical or literary figure—one was William Shakespeare—and each purchased by a different collector. Can you deduce which mug each woman bought and how much she paid for it?

1. Greta spent $250 of the $1300 total spent by all five.

2. Inez spent twice as much as the buyer of the Sherlock Holmes mug, who spent $50 more than Hazel.

3. The Ebenezer Scrooge mug cost more than the one Joan bought.

4. No two collectors spent the same amount.

5. Fran spent $50 more than the one who bought the Henry VIII mug.

6. Hazel did not buy the Winston Churchill mug.

7. The one who bought the Scrooge mug did not spend the second-most money.

8. Fran did not buy the Holmes mug.

9. Inez did not purchase the Henry VIII mug.

The solution is on page 159.

woman	price	mug

53 THE GARDENERS

by Mary A. Powell

Ms. Gardner and four other retired people in Zionsburg are active gardeners. While they work in their yards, they enjoy frequent visits from the five children who live in the neighborhood. One week, each gardener had an abundance of one particular type of flower and was delighted to share it with the children. As it turned out, each child visited a different gardener each weekday (Monday–Friday), and each gardener was visited by a different child each day that week. From the following clues, can you find the last name of each gardener, the type of flower each shared (one shared yellow tulips), and the first name of the child that visited each gardener each day?

1. Tommy visited these three in consecutive order: Ms. Moss, Mr. Flowers, and the one who gave him purple grape hyacinths.

2. Ms. Bloom saw no boys on Wednesday.

3. The person who shared yellow daffodils saw the three boys on consecutive days.

4. Sarah was given purple and white violets on Tuesday; Kevin received pink plum blossoms on Friday.

5. Betsy received yellow flowers two days in a row.

6. Kevin visited Mr. Waters the day before Sarah did.

7. Johnny visited men on Monday and Tuesday; Tommy visited a woman on Thursday.

8. Sarah received daffodils the day before Tommy did, which was two days before Kevin received violets.

The solution is on page 159.

CHILDREN

	Monday	Tuesday	Wednesday	Thursday	Friday
Ms. Bloom (flower)					
Mr. Flowers (flower)					
Ms. Gardner (flower)					
Ms. Moss (flower)					
Mr. Waters (flower)					

FLOWERS

	Mon.	Tues.	Wed.	Thurs.	Fri.
Betsy					
Johnny					
Kevin					
Sarah					
Tommy					

54 COMMUNITY COLLEGE COURSES

by Nancy R. Patterson

Ms. Wright and three friends each signed up for two courses at Excelsior Community College this term. With the help of the clues below, can you figure out each woman's full name and program?

1. Ms. Jackson attends one course with Donna and another with Vicky.

2. Donna and Ms. Kane take only evening courses, but Carolyn and the only one who takes car maintenance each take at least one daytime course.

3. The only one to take accounting also takes oil painting.

4. Ms. Moore attends one course with Laura.

5. At least one of the women takes aerobics, which meets only in the evenings, and at least one takes decorating.

The solution is on page 160.

Note: This Problem is harder than it looks. Use this space for solving.

55 THE BABY-SITTER

by Julie Spence

LeAnn Jones is the most popular baby-sitter in Bloomsville. Last October, LeAnn baby-sat every Saturday night (the first was October 2nd) for a different couple; each couple hired her for a different number of hours (one hired her for five hours). LeAnn was paid $1.00 an hour, and she earned a total of $20.00 for these five Saturday nights. From the information below, can you determine the full names of each couple LeAnn baby-sat for (one husband is Paul), the date she sat for each, and for how many hours?

1. Two of the couples, Bob and his wife and the Trumans, each have two children.

2. LeAnn baby-sat for Gary and his wife twice as many hours as she did for the Thompsons.

3. LeAnn baby-sat for John and his wife three weeks earlier than for Sue and her husband, who do not have precisely two children.

4. The McNeils, who have more than one child, hired LeAnn the weekend immediately preceding the weekend LeAnn sat for Mary and her husband.

5. LeAnn baby-sat for Carol and her husband twice as many hours as she did for the Adelsons, who have three children.

6. Amy and her husband have more children than the couple LeAnn sat for on October 16th, but fewer than Mark and his wife or the Browns.

7. Judy and her husband, who have only one child, hired LeAnn for 3 hours.

The solution is on page 161.

The solution is on page 161.

BABY-SITTING SCHEDULE	HRS.
Oct. 2	
Oct. 9	
Oct. 16	
Oct. 23	
Oct. 30	

56 BUS DRIVERS

by Mary A. Powell

Lyons and four other school bus drivers have a regular route from the bus yard to the high school and back. From the following clues, can you find the full name of each driver, the order in which each left the bus yard, the order in which each returned, and the number of students each carried?

1. All drivers carried more than 35 students, and no two carried the same number.

2. The five drivers are Lois, the one who left first, the one who returned last, Miller, and the driver with 50 students.

3. Owens left before Darlene, but returned after; King left before Charles, but returned after. The fifth driver had 60 passengers. (All five are mentioned here.)

4. Jane, who was second to return, had 10 more passengers than Newberry and 5 more than Henry.

5. The driver who returned third had 5 more passengers than the one who left third and 15 more passengers than the one who left second.

6. Newberry did not have 60 passengers; Miller had an odd number.

7. Darlene did not leave last.

The solution is on page 161.

		King	Lyons	Miller	Newberry	Owens	out					back				
							1	2	3	4	5	1	2	3	4	5
Darlene																
Lois																
Jane																
Charles																
Henry																
back	1															
	2															
	3															
	4															
	5															
out	1															
	2															
	3															
	4															
	5															

OUT

1_____

2_____

3_____

4_____

5_____

BACK

1_____

2_____

3_____

4_____

5_____

57 PHYSICAL ACTIVITY CLASSES

by Randall L. Whipkey

As part of its community recreation program, Cozy Valley offers ten different activity courses each given once per week. The courses are scheduled two per evening, Monday through Friday, one from 6:00 to 8:00 and the other from 8:00 to 10:00. Each of the five Smith children is enrolled in two of the classes, with no two children taking any of the same courses. From the following clues, can you deduce the two courses each child is taking, as well as when each course is held?

1. None of the children is taking two classes the same night.

2. Both Linda and Jane take their two courses before Bob and Rick have either of theirs.

3. The judo course is held earlier the same evening as Jane takes one of her classes, while the floor-exercise class is the same evening as one of Bob's.

4. The volleyball, squash, and ballet courses, in that chronological order (but not necessarily consecutively), are held earlier in the week than the karate course.

5. Bob has his two courses on consecutive days; Jane does not.

6. Pete has one course the same night as the balance-beam class is held and his other course later the same evening as one of Rick's courses.

7. The floor-exercise class is held earlier in the week than the handball course which is held earlier in the week than table tennis.

8. Karate is Thursday from 6:00 to 8:00.

9. Rick takes neither tumbling nor handball.

10. Squash and table tennis have the same time period on different nights.

The solution is on page 162.

The solution is on page 162.

	Mon.	Tues.	Wed.	Thurs.	Fri.
6:00–8:00					
8:00–10:00					

102

58 NEW FENCES

by Diane Yoko

Because of a recent storm in the town of Cloverville, Greg and his wife and four other couples were forced to replace their damaged fences; one couple chose the shadow box type. From the following clues, can you pair up the couples, determine where each lives and the style of fence each chose, and figure out how many feet of fencing each couple needed?

1. The chain-link fence is half the footage of the scalloped fence but twice the footage of the one of Tilmon Street, which is not the stockade fence.

2. The couple living on Cline Street did not need the most fencing.

3. John and his wife, who is neither Theresa nor Sandy, needed more feet of fencing than at least one other couple.

4. Sandy and her husband live on Wright Street. Their fence is 15 feet shorter than the chain-link, and half the length of the one that Bob and his wife erected.

5. Neither Michelle nor Lynn lives on Jay Street; Michelle isn't Bob's wife.

6. The basket-weave fence on Elmer Street is not the smallest of the five.

7. Joyce and her husband needed the smallest fence, with 70 feet of fence.

8. Warren and his wife, who is not Joyce, needed less fencing than Albert and his wife.

The solution is on page 162.

Use this space for solving.

59 BOOK BONANZA

by Susan Zivich

The Davis child and the other eight children in Gwen Boyer's third-grade class reported that they had read a total of forty-five books over the last summer vacation. Each child had read at least one book and, oddly enough, no two children had read the same number of books. From the following clues, can you determine each child's full name, the number of books each read, as well as the seating plan of the class?

1. Larry read twice as many books as the child who sits to his immediate right.

2. The three children in the middle row are (in no particular order) Al, the Lotak child, and the child who read three books.

3. The Redeagle child read as many books as the two children behind her in her row did together.

4. Bill sits directly in front of the Baer child and to Fred's left.

5. The three children in the left row (the children's left) are (in no particular order) Mary, the Peterson child, and the child who read two books.

6. Paul read seven books.

7. No child has the same first and last initials.

8. The Adams child, who read four books, is not the last child in his or her row.

9. The three children who read the fewest books are (in no particular order) Debbie, Regina, and the Evans child.

10. The Martin child read three times as many books as the child directly in front of him or her.

11. The three children in the right row (the children's right) are (in no particular order) Eleanor, the Fedirka child, and the child who read one book.

The solution is on page 163.

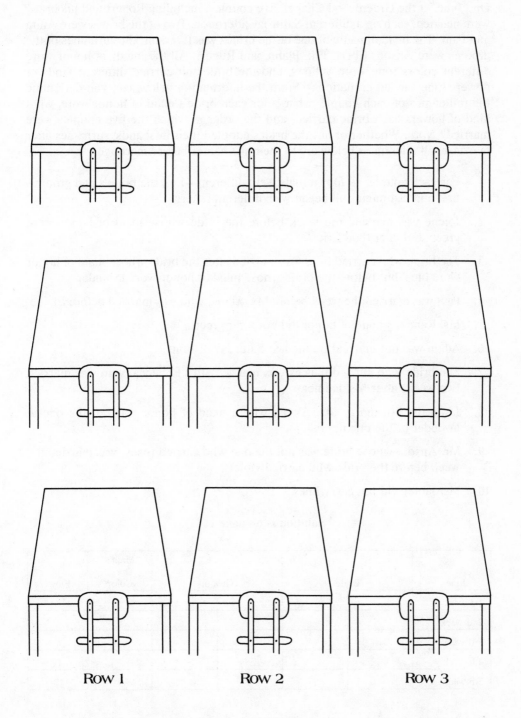

Row 1   Row 2   Row 3

60 FIVE WEDDINGS IN JUNE

by Julie Spence

One June, at the Greenwood Chapel, five couples, including Robert and his bride, were married, each on a different Saturday afternoon. Two of the brides were Anita and Pam. The maiden name of one of the brides was Everson; the surnames of the grooms were Anson, Ebert, Jilk, Plahn, and Rupert. All the maids of honor wore different colors (one wore yellow), and the brides all carried different kinds of flowers (one carried carnations). From the information below, can you determine the full names of each couple, what color each bride's maid of honor wore, what kind of flowers each bride carried, and the order in which the five couples were married? *Note:* Whether or not the brides adopted their husbands' surnames after marriage, all references below are to their last names before marriage.

1. For each couple, all four initials were different—i.e., the bride's and groom's first and last names all began with different letters.

2. Jolene was married the week before the bride whose maid of honor wore green, but later than Eric.

3. The bride who carried lilies was married after the bride whose maid of honor wore blue, but before the bride whose maid of honor wore lavender.

4. Paul was married the week before Ms. Akins, who was married before Elaine.

5. Ms. Ranner's maid of honor did not wear green.

6. Adam was not married on the last Saturday in June.

7. The bride who carried daisies was married after Rebecca, who was married two weeks after Ms. Palmer.

8. Jason did not marry Ms. Akins, whose maid of honor was not the one in lavender or the one in pink.

9. Mr. Anson, whose bride was not the one who carried roses, was married the week before the bride who carried violets.

10. Ms. Jabley did not carry lilies.

Solution is on page 164.

Solution is on page 164.

June	Bride	Groom	Maid's Dress Color	Flowers
1st week				
2nd week				
3rd week				
4th week				
5th week				

61 THE MOUNTAINEERS

by Ellen K. Rodehorst

In the history of mountaineering, Mr. Amadeo and five other men are among the distinguished group of men and women who first succeeded in climbing to the summit of a challenging mountain. These six men led expeditions in different countries, including Nepal, to ascend peaks of different altitudes; one is 11,342 feet, another is 16,795 feet. The expeditions each took place in a different year, beginning in 1880; one expedition climbed Chimbarazo Peak. From the facts given below, can you determine each mountaineer's full name (one man's first name is Martin), the name, location, and altitude of the peak he climbed, and the year in which he ascended it?

1. Luigi, who isn't Mr. Conway, ascended one of the peaks, which isn't the one in Ecuador, six years before Mt. Sir Sandford was climbed.
2. Three of the mountaineers, Maurice, Mr. Palmer, and the man who climbed the Pakistani peak, all undertook their expeditions at least thirty-two years after the first of the six expeditions conquered the 20,702-foot peak.
3. Margherita Peak was named by the mountaineer (not Mr. Hertzog) who succeeded in climbing it in 1906.
4. The most recent expedition of the six took place forty-one years after another man climbed to the summit of the Canadian peak.
5. The 26,660-foot peak was conquered in 1953.
6. Hermann's last name is not Hertzog and his expedition, which took place after 1900, was not the one to Annapurna's summit, which is not the Ugandan peak.
7. The expedition led by Mr. Buhl occurred three years after one of the other men reached the summit of the 26,391-foot peak.
8. Nanga Parbat's summit was successfully climbed several decades after Mr. Conway led his expedition to Bolivia.
9. The ascent to the summit of the 21,184-foot peak occurred fourteen years before Howard climbed the Canadian peak.
10. Among the six expeditions, the lowest peak was climbed fourth and the highest peak was climbed last.
11. Edward was not the one who first climbed to the summit of Illimani.
12. Mr. Whymper was well known for his climb at least twenty years before the man who climbed Mt. Sir Sandford began his expedition.
13. Maurice was not the leader of the expedition in Ecuador.
14. Annapurna's summit is higher than the 21,184-foot peak, which is not the mountain Edward climbed.

The solution is on page 164.

Hint: We found it most helpful to establish chronology first.

year	mountain climber		mountain	location	altitude
	first name	last name			

62 BALLOON RACE

by Mary A. Powell

David and four other commercial balloon pilots held an impromptu race one morning, with each pilot taking along one passenger; one took his mother. From the following clues, can you find each pilot's full name, his balloon's color, each passenger's full name (one first name is Alice, one last name Loomis) and relationship to the pilot, and the positions of the five balloons in the race? (*Note:* The married women mentioned in this problem have adopted their husbands' surnames.)

1. Pilot King and the pilot in the green and gold balloon are the only two of the five who are single; neither is the pilot who came in second. The blue and white balloon did not come in second. Ms. Queen, who is not Esther, was the only single passenger.

2. The purple and gold balloon landed after the balloon George piloted, but before the one in which Mr. Patterson was a passenger. Of the other two, pilot Jones (who didn't land last) landed immediately after the balloon in which the pilot's wife was a passenger.

3. The pilot who took his fiancée was not pilot Charles.

4. Robert and Susan both enjoyed their first balloon rides with their brothers.

5. At least three balloons landed before the red and white one.

6. The balloon Edward was piloting came in after the one in which Baker was a passenger but before the green and red balloon.

7. Patricia waved to her husband, who watched from the ground.

8. Pilot Maloney (who is not Frank) did not come in second. Frank, who has owned his balloon for years, is married.

The solution is on page 165.

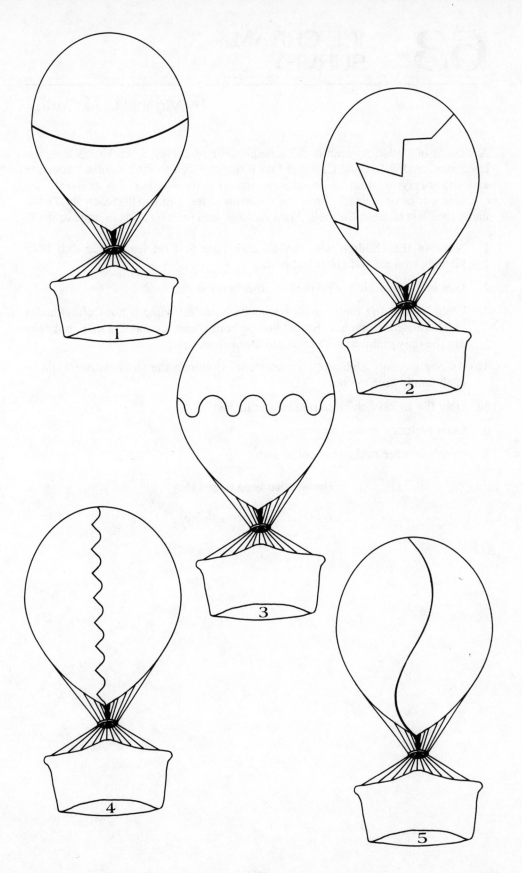

63 ICE-CREAM SURVEY

by Virginia C. McCarthy

A student of statistics recently did a neighborhood survey on children's tastes in ice cream, asking Iris and Carl and four other children to rank vanilla, chocolate and strawberry in order of preference, and to state whether they preferred ice cream in a cone or in a dish. From the following clues, can you find each child's full name (one last name is Carmel), flavor ranking, and preference as to cone or dish?

1. None of the children who ranked chocolate first (at least three did) have siblings who ranked chocolate first.

2. Ivan is the only child who ranked strawberry first.

3. Craig (who didn't rank vanilla last and whose last name is not Coffey) and a child whose last name is Rippel do not both prefer a cone to a dish, but they are the only children with identical flavor rankings.

4. Among the only children, all prefer cones; among the siblings, one child in each family prefers cones.

5. Only the Brickel children ranked vanilla last.

6. Celia prefers a dish to a cone.

7. Irene's brother ranked chocolate last.

The solution is on page 165.

Use this space for solving.

TRUE-FALSE
QUIZ

by Evelyn Rosenthal

To offset the effect of guessing, true-false tests are often scored by subtracting the number of wrong answers from the number of right ones, with omitted items not counted. Recently, a 30-item true-false test, so scored, was given in which Bill, Dot, and six other students all got the same score, although no two of them answered the same number of questions. All eight belong to at least two of the five student clubs at their high school, but no two belong to exactly the same combination of clubs. From the following clues, can you find the full name of each student (one last name is Mills), the clubs to which each belongs, the number of questions each answered correctly and incorrectly, and the score they each got?

1. Neither Paul, who is not the Ross boy, nor Al was the one who had no wrong answers.

2. No one belongs to both the Hiking and the Stamp Club, or to both the Model Railroad and the Chess Club.

3. The four Drama Club members answered the largest number of items.

4. No one had more than seven incorrect answers.

5. The Evans youngster, who belongs to the Model Railroad Club but not the Drama Club, answered more questions than anyone else who is not a member of the Drama Club.

6. Grace and the Leroy girl answered fewer items than the other Drama Club members.

7. Mike and the North girl between them represent all five clubs and have no club membership in common; the same is true of Paul and the Fisher youngster.

8. Of the Drama Club members, the two who also belong to the Model Railroad Club answered more questions than the two who also belong to the Chess Club.

9. The Clark girl, who answered 20 questions, and Karen, who answered 26, belong to two of the same clubs.

10. Of those who do not belong to the Drama Club, the two in the Hiking Club answered more items than the two in the Stamp Club.

11. Joe, who answered 28 questions (which was not the most), and the Horn youngster, who answered 18, belong to two of the same clubs.

The solution is on page 166.

Use this space for solving.

65 PETS ALLOWED— NO VACANCY

by Cheryl L. McLaughlin

Sue and her husband live in the only apartment building on Center Street that allows pets. The building consists of three floors, with apartments A, B, and C on each floor; the B apartment on each floor is the middle one. Each of the nine married couples in the building, including the Willises, owns a dog, a bird, or a cat; one pet's name is Frenchie. No two couples living on the same floor or in the same vertical line have the same kind of pet. From the following clues, can you determine each couple's full names (one husband is Tony), apartment, kind of pet, and pet's name? (*Note:* You may assume that all the women have adopted their husbands' surnames.)

1. The Carters, who own a bird, live in the apartment directly below Kim and her husband (who isn't Pete) and next door to George and his wife, who have a pet named Twinkle.

2. Mr. Davis (who isn't Tim) and his wife on the third floor, Bob and his wife Ann on the second floor, and the couple who own Tiny (who aren't the Harrises) all own dogs; neither the Davises' nor Bob's and Ann's pet is the one named Peanuts.

3. The Fields live between, and on the same floor as, the couple who own Cleo the cat and Mike and his wife; Phil and his wife Kate live directly above the Fields, and Gina and her husband live directly below.

4. Marie and her husband, who aren't the Adamses, live directly above the couple who own Peppy and next door to Mr. and Mrs. Mills.

5. Tom and his wife, who aren't the Harrises, live on a higher floor than Jim and his wife, who own a pet named Chipper; Tom's pet, Fluffy, isn't a dog.

6. Cathy Burk and her husband live in apartment 2C.

7. Martha and her husband, who isn't Pete, live directly above the Joneses; Martha's pet isn't the one named Pepper.

8. Sally and her husband do not own a dog.

The solution is on page 167.

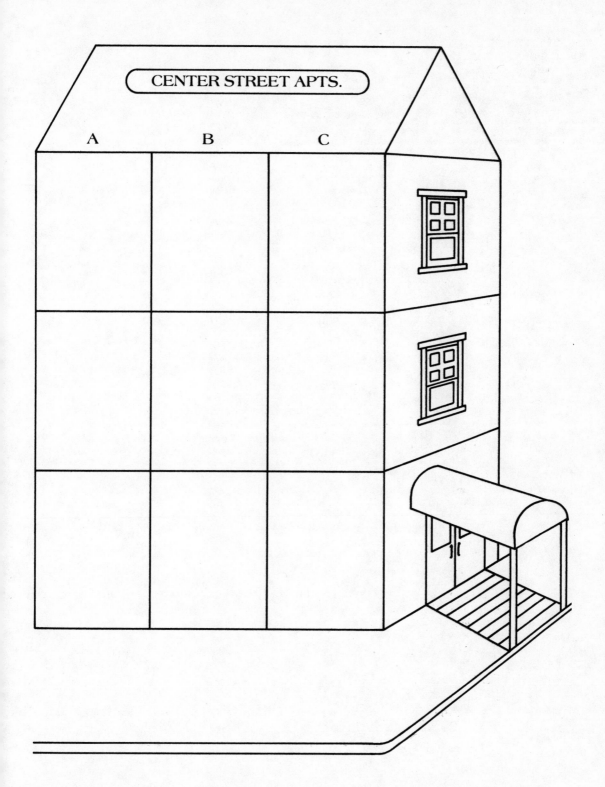

CENTER STREET APTS.

A   B   C

CHALLENGER LOGIC PROBLEMS

66 HOMECOMING DAY

by Evelyn Rosenthal

On Homecoming Day at a four-year college, Kalb and four other graduates lined up to buy school pennants. From the following clues, can you find the full name, occupation (one is a banker), graduation year, and place in line of each?

1. Jay, who was first in line, graduated in 1946.

2. Carl, who is not Larsen, graduated five years after the lawyer.

3. Dot graduated four years after Jackson.

4. Irons graduated five years after the engineer.

5. Hollis was ahead of at least two others in line.

6. The teacher, who is not Rose, was fifth in line and graduated in 1956.

7. Sam was not fifth in line, but he was behind the physician.

8. While no two of the five were in the same class or in consecutive classes, every two who stood next to each other in line had been in college together at the same time for at least one year.

The solution is on page 167.

The solution is on page 167.

place in line	year graduated	first name	last name	occupation
1				
2				
3				
4				
5				

117

67 FROM CORDIALITY TO FRIENDLYTOWN

by Margaret Shoop

One afternoon, five cars of different colors, including a red one, left one after the other to make the trip from Cordiality to Friendlytown. Two of the drivers were Ms. Palmer and Mr. Moore. They arrived in Friendlytown in a different order than they left Cordiality, as a result of four occasions when one car passed another. (Only these five cars were on the road between the two towns that afternoon.) From the clues that follow, can you determine the owner of each car; the order in which they left Cordiality; the order in which they arrived in Friendlytown; and who passed whom, in what order, during the trip?

1. The tan car, which was not driven by Mr. O'Brien, did not pass any of the other cars, nor was it passed by any of them.
2. Ms. Lyons, who didn't drive the gray car, was in the lead leaving Cordiality but was the next-to-last to arrive in Friendlytown.
3. The woman driving the blue car was in the lead for part of the trip but was not in the lead either leaving Cordiality or arriving in Friendlytown.
4. The second and third passings were done by Ms. Nichols and the driver of the cream-colored car, not necessarily in that order.
5. Ms. Nichols was not the next-to-last driver to leave Cordiality.

The solution is on page 168.

leaving Cordiality	after 1st pass	after 2nd pass	after 3rd pass	after 4th pass order arriving in Friendlytown
1.				
2.				
3.				
4.				
5.				

68 HOME IMPROVEMENTS

by Margaret Shoop

The five families who live on the north side of the 100 block of Sunny Avenue all recently made major improvements in their homes; one family installed central air-conditioning. The five houses are numbered 101 through 109, from west to east. From the clues that follow, can you determine the color of each house, which family lives in each, and what improvements each family made?

1. The Kilmers live next door to the white house where a family room was added.

2. The Longs live next door to, and east of, the house where a garage was added.

3. The Jensen family and the Holt family live two doors apart; the Jensens live next door to the Gellers' yellow house.

4. The house at #107 is buff.

5. The two white houses are not next door to each other; and only one of the two is an end house.

6. Neither the Geller family nor the family at #101 are the ones who redid their kitchen.

7. The red house is two doors from the one where the attic was finished.

8. The Holts are not the ones who added a family room.

The solution is on page 169.

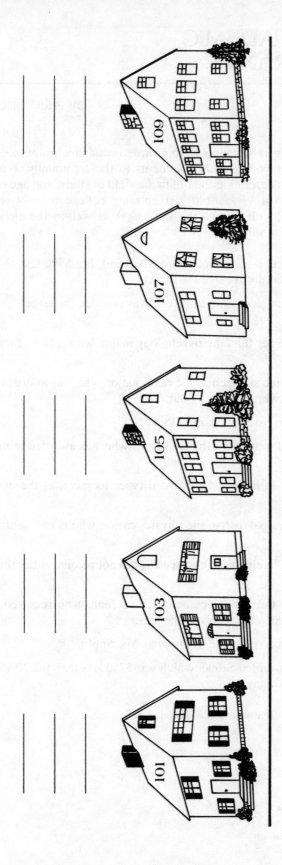

SUNNY AVENUE

69 ACADEMIC GRANTS

by Julie Spence

This past spring, the Baldwin Women's Club awarded academic grants to Debra and seven other promising young women students in the community. From the information below, can you determine the full name, field of study, and age of each recipient (they range from a 17-year-old just entering college to a 24-year-old pursuing graduate studies, with no two the same age), as well as the amount of each award (no two were the same)?

1. Ms. Nelson was awarded $500 more than Ms. Lind, but $500 less than the history major (who did not receive the most).

2. Mary, who is two years older than Ms. Cole, was awarded the largest amount, $3500.

3. Mandy is two years older than the psychology major, who is two years older than Ms. Mack.

4. Amy was awarded twice as much as the math major, who was awarded twice as much as Ms. Vail, who is 22 years old.

5. Ms. Smith is five years younger than Nikki.

6. Ms. Fox was awarded more than the art major, who was awarded more than Barbara.

7. The one who majors in music was awarded twice as much as the one who majors in English.

8. Ms. Jones is two years older than the physics major, who is two years older than Candy.

9. The student majoring in electrical engineering did not receive either the most or least.

10. The 21-year-old was awarded twice as much as Jean, who received $1500 more than the recipient who received the least.

11. The physics major received twice as much as Ms. Smith.

12. The 23-year-old was awarded $1000, which was $750 less than the 20-year-old and $1000 less than Mandy.

The solution is on page 169.

$	first name	last name	age	major

17	18	19	20	21	22	23	24

123

70 BATTER UP

by Cheryl L. McLaughlin

At season's end, all the boys on a championship baseball team had different numbers of home runs and strike-outs; none had more than nine of either, and each boy had at least one of each. From the following clues, can you determine each boy's full name, number of home runs and strike-outs, and position on the team? *Note:* The positions on the baseball team are: pitcher; catcher; shortstop; the three basemen—first, second, and third; and the three outfielders—right, left, and center.

1. The three basemen—who are Mike (whose last name isn't Day), Billy, and Steve—had a total of nine home runs; the first baseman was the only boy on the team with an equal number of home runs and strike-outs.

2. The Lentz boy, who doesn't play second base, had six fewer home runs and four fewer strike-outs than Robby, who doesn't play in the outfield; Robby had two fewer home runs than the Stone boy, who isn't the catcher; Mike had one more strike-out than the Lentz boy.

3. Ed Price, the shortstop, had five home runs and eight strike-outs.

4. Matt, who is neither the pitcher nor an outfielder, had six more home runs than the Day boy, who isn't Steve; the Day boy had five more strike-outs than Jim, who didn't have the least.

5. The Burk boy had the most strike-outs; the Moore boy, who isn't Tim, struck out four times.

6. The Miller boy had twice as many home runs as Tim, who had one more strike-out than the center fielder.

7. The Sand boy isn't the right fielder.

8. The Hoyt boy had twice as many home runs as Joey.

The solution is on page 170.

HOME RUNS

first name	last name	position	# of HR's

STRIKE-OUTS

first name	last name	position	# of SO's

71   BILLY AND THE PETS

by Mary A. Powell

Five-year-old Billy was delighted when a neighbor's cat had five black kittens, and he visited every day to pet the mama cat and her babies. One day, before his visit, he took his two dogs for a walk around the block and counted all the pets. "There are six houses on this block," he announced to his neighbor, "and every house has at least one pet. There are fifteen cats, including kittens, and six dogs; one of the dogs is a puppy." The locations of the six homes, occupied by the Canfields and five other families, are shown on the accompanying map; all the lots are divided from one another by fences. From the following clues, can you find each family's address and the number, kinds, and colors of their pets? (*Note:* While *side-by-side* neighbors face the same street, *adjacent* neighbors may share either a side fence or a back fence.)

1. The Jacksons' big orange cat is friendly with the two old orange cats who live in another house, but he doesn't like the two old black male cats who also live there.

2. All but one household have at least one cat or kitten; all but one household have at least one dog or puppy; only four households have at least one black cat or kitten.

3. The two families with the most pets live as far apart as possible; one family has two more pets than the other.

4. The Allens, who do not live at 104 Elm Street, have no young pets.

5. Billy's family has two more pets than the family with the fewest and four fewer than the family with the most.

6. The Smiths' pets are the same color; their only kitten likes to play with the Kings' red dog.

7. The Bakers, who do not live on Maple Street, have an old gray male cat; one of their two adjacent neighbors has a collie; their only other neighbor, a tiny black puppy.

8. The two white dogs live side by side; one lives with a calico cat; the other with a brown dog.

9. The litter of kittens, who do not live at 105 Maple Street, look exactly like their father and grandmother, who live in a house adjacent to them.

The solution is on page 171.

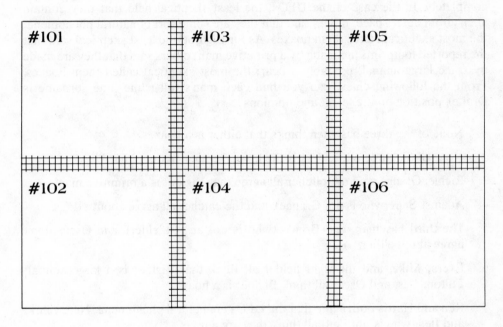

Maple Street

#101   #103   #105

#102   #104   #106

Elm Street

72 BIGFOOT AND UFOs

by Evelyn Rosenthal

During a rain delay, Tony and the other eight members of a baseball team whiled away the time in the dugout by arguing about Bigfoot and UFOs. Opinions varied from the least to the most skeptical on each, and no two of the players agreed completely. In the case of the UFOs, the least skeptical held that they contain aliens from outer space; others said that they are some sort of natural phenomena; the most skeptical called them hoaxes. As for Bigfoot, the least skeptical said that the reported footprints are made by a primitive man; others said that they are made by some large animal, probably a bear; the most skeptical called them hoaxes. From the following clues, can you find each man's full name (one surname is Drake), position on the team, and opinions?

1. None of the three basemen thinks that either is a hoax.

2. None of the three outfielders is the least skeptical about either.

3. Richie, Grange, and the pitcher all agree that Bigfoot is a primitive man.

4. Adams, Sam (who is not Grange), and the catcher all agree about UFOs.

5. The third baseman, and Brown (who is not an outfielder), and Oscar don't agree about either.

6. Evers, Mike, and the right fielder all think that Bigfoot is a large animal; Fulton, Les, and Oscar all think Bigfoot is a hoax.

7. Ken and Harris both agree that the UFOs are natural phenomena; Ned, Clark, and Iles (who is not Phil) all think they are a hoax.

8. The shortstop does not hold either the most or the least skeptical opinion on either Bigfoot or UFOs.

9. The left fielder, right fielder, and third baseman all disagree about both; so do the second baseman, Fulton, and Phil.

The solution is on page 172.

	UFOs		
	least skeptical ALIENS	NATURAL PHENOMENON	most skeptical HOAX
least skeptical PRIMITIVE MAN			
LARGE ANIMAL			
most skeptical HOAX			

73   ZIONSBURG NEIGHBORS

by Mary A. Powell

A city block in Zionsburg is occupied by Carol, Edna, George, and their five neighbors. Each has a fruit tree, a vegetable garden, and a flower garden which produce so abundantly that there is enough to share with all the other neighbors. All eight neighbors enjoy a variety, since the fruit trees are all different, and all grow different vegetables (one grows asparagus) and flowers (one woman grows marigolds). Four of the neighbors live on the north side of the block, the other four on the south side; the four corner houses, however, face either east or west, as shown in the diagram given. The lots are separated by fences or hedges; they have been numbered only for convenience. From the following clues, can you determine each lot owner's full name (one surname is Long) and the type of fruit, flower, and vegetable each grows? (*Note:* "Between," as used below, describes the middle house of three adjacent homes in a straight line. Also, tomatoes have been considered a vegetable.)

1. None of the eight has a first or last name with the same initial letter as any of the items he or she grows.

2. The homes of the man with the plum tree and the man who raises lettuce both face north; those of Ms. Nelson and the person who raises irises both face west; those of Helen and the person who raises peas both face east; those of Mr. Queen and the cabbage grower both face south.

3. David and Mr. King both live between a man and a woman; Fred lives between two women; Ms. Jones lives between two men.

4. These two pairs of neighbors live as far apart as possible: Mr. Owens and Ms. Powers and the potato grower and Betty.

5. Neither the tulip grower nor the daffodil grower raises beans.

6. Mr. Macy chats over his back fence with the man who raises zucchini, who does not have a peach tree.

7. The homes of the lemon grower and the orange grower face in the same direction.

8. The camellia grower and the woman who raises carnations are on adjacent lots, but their homes do not face in the same direction.

9. The apple grower lives between the peach grower and the pear grower.

10. The apricot grower, the tomato grower, the rose grower, and the bean grower are the four who live on the north side of the block.

11. Adam, whose home does not face east or west, lives between the cherry grower and the gladiola grower.

12. No two items grown on the same lot begin with the same letter.

The solution is on page 173.

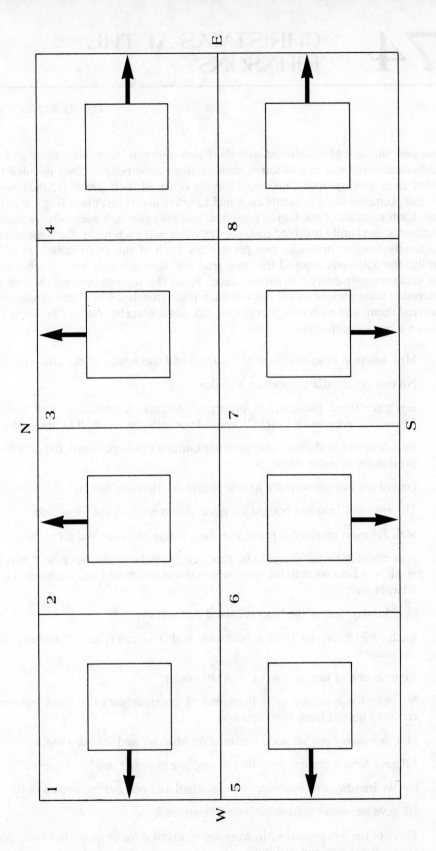

74 CHRISTMAS AT THE JOHNSONS'

by Julie Spence

One year Mr. and Mrs. Johnson and their four children, John, Jim, Jane, and Jill, celebrated Christmas in a different manner from most people. They decided that rather than waiting until Christmas Day to open all their presents, they would instead exchange some presents each night for five nights just preceding Christmas Day. Each member of the family gave one, and only one, gift each night, and each member of the family received one, and only one, gift each night. Each member of the family bought, or made, one present for each of the other members of the family. The Johnsons enjoyed this new tradition so much they have celebrated in the same manner every Christmas since. From the information below, can you determine what presents were opened each night that first Christmas season, who received them, and who gave them? One gift was a bracelet. *Note:* Christmas Day was on a Saturday that year.

1. Mrs. Johnson is an excellent seamstress and she sewed all the gifts she gave.

2. No one received a sweater on Monday.

3. Jim gave these presents, in order: a necklace, hairbrushes, golf balls, a Christmas plate and a baseball. He did not give the baseball to his mother.

4. Jane, who is not the one who gave her father a cribbage board, did give him a present on Monday night.

5. One of the boys received a jigsaw puzzle on Thursday night.

6. The gifts Mr. Johnson bought for his children were all the same item.

7. Mrs. Johnson received a purse two days before she received a candle.

8. Jane could not wear the gift she received Thursday night, because it was too small; she later went to the store where it was purchased and exchanged it for a larger size.

9. On Monday, one of the boys received a model car.

10. Each child received both a bathrobe and a sweater; no other gifts were duplicated.

11. Jill gave one of her brothers a football poster.

12. Mr. Johnson received a tie from one of his daughters two days before he received his gift from Mrs. Johnson.

13. Mrs. Johnson gave her sons presents on Monday and Tuesday nights.

14. Jill gave John a present two days before she gave her mother a present.

15. On Wednesday, one boy received a softball and one girl received a doll.

16. Jill gave her sister bubble bath on Christmas Eve.

17. Three of the five presents Mr. Johnson received were, in no particular order, a shirt, aftershave, and golf balls.

18. Mrs. Johnson received a pair of earrings from John and perfume from one of her other children.

19. Jim received a magic set after Jane received a Monopoly game.

20. One child had no trouble guessing what the present from Mrs. Johnson was, because all the other children had received the same item from her earlier in the week.

The solution is on page 174.

	Mom gave	Dad gave	John gave	Jim gave	Jane gave	Jill gave
Mon.						
Tues.						
Wed.						
Thurs.						
Fri.						

	Mom rec.	Dad rec.	John rec.	Jim rec.	Jane rec.	Jill rec.
Mon.						
Tues.						
Wed.						
Thurs.						
Fri.						

75 THE MERCHANTS' CHRISTMAS DECORATIONS

by Evelyn Rosenthal

A group of merchants want to put up uniform Christmas decorations on their block, but they cannot agree about color or design; the possibilities are bells, festoons, stars, or wreaths, in gold, green, red, or silver. The business establishments are #1 to #16, with the numbering beginning at the west end of the block and the odd numbers on the north side, as shown in the accompanying diagram. From the following clues, can you find each merchant's location, color and design preference?

1. All the merchants on the north side of the street agree about gold and silver; i.e., either they all want gold or silver, or none wants gold or silver.

2. Each merchant wants a different combination of color and design; e.g., the only one who wants silver wreaths is the owner of the hardware store at #10.

3. Among them, the owners of the four establishments at the west end of the block want all designs except stars and all colors except gold.

4. The men's and women's clothing stores are directly opposite each other; one owner wants gold and the other green.

5. The owners of the toy store and the children's clothing store, which are adjacent, want different colors; one wants stars.

6. The two pairs of businesses that are farthest apart are the florist and the vegetable store, and the butcher and the bank; no two of the four want the same color or the same decoration.

7. Among them, the owners of the four middle establishments want all designs and colors.

8. The butcher, who doesn't want silver, agrees with the bookstore owner in one respect and with the luncheonette owner in the other; the fish-store owner, who doesn't want bells, also agrees with the bookstore owner in one respect.

9. The middle businesses are the deli and the toy store on one side of the street and the hardware store and the luncheonette on the other.

10. The owners of the businesses at #5, #6, #7, and #8 all want different colors.

11. The drug and shoe stores are directly opposite each other; the hardware store owner agrees with the owner of the drugstore about color and with the owner of the shoe store about design.

12. Two of the clothing stores are adjacent.

13. The hardware store is not next to the stationery store but is closer to it than to the drugstore. All three are on the same side of the street.

14. The vegetable store, whose owner wants wreaths, is next to the women's clothing store.

The solution is on page 175.

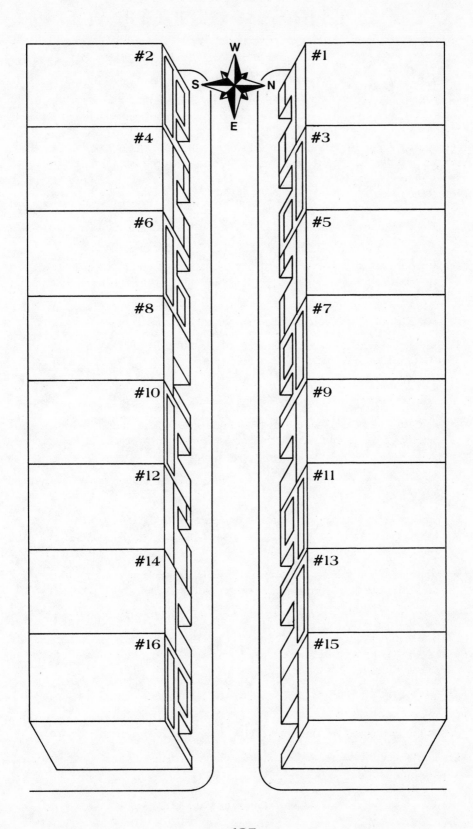

SOLUTIONS

1. LOGICAL FEAST

A woman is bringing the tossed salad (clue 4), but she is not Taffy (clue 3); she is Carmela. Frank is not bringing the green-bean casserole (clue 1) or the cheesecake (clue 5); he is bringing the lasagna. Taffy is not bringing the cheesecake (clue 5), so Sam is, and by elimination, Taffy is bringing the green-bean casserole. Since Ms. Bacon is on a diet (clue 2), she is not Carmela, the woman described in clue 4, who is bringing the tossed salad; Taffy is Ms. Bacon. Carmela isn't Rice (clue 4) or Baker since that last name belongs to a man (clue 2). Carmela is Ms. Cook. Sam is not Rice (clue 4), so he is Mr. Baker and, by elimination, Frank is Mr. Rice. In summary:

> Taffy Bacon, green-bean casserole
> Sam Baker, cheesecake
> Carmela Cook, tossed salad
> Frank Rice, lasagna

2. BRAGGIN'

By lines 9 and 10, the boys are 7, 8, 9, and 10 years of age. Three overstated their ages, and one told the truth (lines 17, 18). Bill's brother is Ben (line 12). Johnny claimed to be 8 (line 13), the age of Bill's brother (lines 15, 16), so Ben is 8 years old. Since Johnny didn't tell the truth, he overstated his age, so his actual age must be 7. By lines 19 and 20, Bill is 9 years old and Max is 10. By line 23, Bill claimed to be 10 years old, and by lines 21 and 22, Max claimed to be 12 years old. Ben must be the one who told the truth. In sum:

> Johnny, age 7, claimed to be 8
> Ben, age 8, told the truth
> Bill, age 9, claimed to be 10
> Max, age 10, claimed to be 12

3. FAMILY NAMES

We know from the introduction that there are four boys in the Jones family and three in the Smith family. Valentine and the twins are brothers and comprise three members of one of the families (clue 1). Benedict and Winston (clue 2) are named after grandfathers; the twins are named after uncles (clue 6), therefore neither Benedict nor Winston is a twin. Benedict is not Valentine's brother (clue 5), so Winston, who is not Benedict's brother (clue 2), must be. Winston, Valentine, and the twins, therefore, are the four Jones children. Briscoe and Hamilton are brothers but cannot be twins (clue 3); therefore they and Benedict must be the three Smith children. By elimination, Decatur and Dewey are the Jones twins, and by clue 4, they are 10 years old. By clue 1, Valentine is 14; by clue 3, Briscoe is 13 and Hamilton 15; by clue 2, Winston is 8, and by clue 5, Benedict is 11. In sum:

> Valentine Jones, 14
> Decatur Jones, 10
> Dewey Jones, 10
> Winston Jones, 8
> Hamilton Smith, 15
> Briscoe Smith, 13
> Benedict Smith, 11

4. APARTMENT PARKING

By clue 4, Mr. White, who isn't Don, must be Frank. Jane, who by clue 5, isn't Logan or Steele, is Ms. Miller. Since the two men, one of whom is Frank White, have end spaces but not end apartments (clue 4), and Logan's apartment and parking space are both somewhere to the left of Jane Miller's and Steele's (clue 5), Logan must be Ann. She lives in apartment A and parks in space #2, and Steele must be Don with the last parking space, # 4. Frank

White, then, has the first space and Jane Miller has apartment D and parking space # 3. By clue 2, then, Frank owns the blue car and Jane the convertible. By clue 3, Ann's car is red and Frank's blue car is the sedan. Frank, then, by clue 1, can't live in apartment C; he lives in B and Don is in C. Ann's red car isn't the hatchback (clue 3); Don's is and Ann's red car is the station wagon. The convertible isn't yellow (clue 2), so it must be green and the hatchback yellow. In sum:

> Ann Logan, apt. A, 2nd space, red station wagon
> Frank White, apt. B, 1st space, blue sedan
> Don Steele, apt. C, 4th space, yellow hatchback
> Jane Miller, apt. D, 3rd space, green convertible

5.   PROM CHAPERONES

The four spouses of the teachers are the pilot (clue 3); Bob, the salesman (clue 4); Amy, the secretary (clue 5); and Rita, the attorney (clue 7). Matt is not a teacher (clue 8), so he must be Mr. White, the pilot (clue 3). Matt's wife teaches science (clue 8). Of the four teachers mentioned in clue 2, his wife can only be Theresa. The English teacher's last name is not Grey or Brown (clue 6), so it is Black. By clue 2, Mr. Grey is a teacher, but not the math teacher, so he teaches art. By elimination, the math teacher's last name is Brown. Mark's last name is not Grey or Brown (clue 2); it is Black, and he is the English teacher. Bob is not a teacher, so he is not Mr. Grey (clue 2); he is Mr. Brown whose wife is the math teacher. Carl, then, is Mr. Grey the art teacher. By elimination, Chris is the math teacher who is married to Bob Brown. Rita is not Mrs. Grey (clue 7), so she is Mrs. Black, and by elimination, Amy is Mrs. Grey. In summary:

> Mark (English teacher) and Rita (attorney) Black
> Chris (math teacher) and Bob (salesman) Brown
> Carl (art teacher) and Amy (secretary) Grey
> Theresa (science teacher) and Matt (pilot) White

6.   STUFFED ANIMALS

By clue 1, the four children are: Cyndi; the three-year-old; the one who received the bunny; and the one who received the blue toy. Also by clue 1, the children opened their toys in the order listed. By clue 4, then, the two-year-old is not the one who received the blue toy, nor is s/he the one who received the bunny just before the blue toy. Cyndi, then, is the two-year-old, and the three-year-old received the red toy (clue 4). The three-year-old did not receive the lamb or, by clue 3, Scott would be two years old, the same as Cyndi (contradicting the introduction). The lamb was not the blue toy (clue 3), so Cyndi received the lamb. Scott, then, is one year old (also clue 3). Since there are four children, each one year older than the other (introduction), and Scott is one year old, he must be the youngest and the oldest would then be four years old. Since s/he didn't receive the blue toy (clue 2), his/her orange animal (again clue 2) must be the bunny. By elimination, Cyndi received the yellow toy. Also by elimination, Scott is the child who received the blue toy. He did not receive the raccoon (clue 3), so he received the hippo, and the three-year-old received the raccoon. The four-year-old is not Robin (clue 2) so she is Jessie, and the three-year-old is Robin. In summary, from youngest to oldest, we have:

> Scott, 1, blue hippo
> Cyndi, 2 yellow lamb
> Robin, 3, red raccoon
> Jessie, 4, orange bunny

7.   A ROUND OF GOLF

Bill scored the lowest (clue 1). The scores ranged between 70 and 85 strokes. Clubb, who scored 10 strokes more than the pro-shop clerk (clue 2), must have scored at least 80. Carter scored 78 and had a higher score than Frank (clue 4), making the order from lowest to highest—Bill, Frank, Carter, and Clubb. Frank is not Sands (clue 3), so he is Green and Bill's last name is Sands. Clubb is not Paul (clue 2) so Carter is, and Clubb is Jack. Bill Sands, who scored the least (clue 1), scored 4 and 7 strokes less than two other players (clue 3). A fourth player scored 10 strokes more than someone else. Therefore, since Paul Carter, who is in third place, scored a 78 (clue 4), Bill must have scored a 71 and Frank Green a 75. Paul must be the caddy mentioned in clue 3. Jack Clubb, who scored 10 points more than someone else (clue 2), then scored either 81 or 85. No one scored 81 (clue 5), so Clubb shot an 85 and Frank is the pro-shop clerk. Bill is not the maintenance man (clue 1), so Jack Clubb is, and Bill, by elimination, is the short-order cook. In sum:

> Paul Carter, caddy, 78
> Jack Clubb, maintenance man, 85
> Frank Green, pro-shop clerk, 75
> Bill Sands, short-order cook, 71

8. SPECIAL ARRIVALS

There are two girls and two boys—a girl and a boy (David and Joy) mentioned in the introduction, Tommy (clue 3) and Molly (clue 4). The boys didn't exit consecutively (clue 2). Neither of the boys—Chang-soo (clue 1) nor Sung-chul (clue 5)—got off first, so the exit order was girl, boy, girl, boy. The girl Yung-hee also wasn't first (clue 3), so Mee-sook was, and Yung-hee was third. By the same clue, Tommy was second and the Potters' son, who must be David, last. By clue 5, Frank's daughter is Yung-hee, Gail's daughter is Mee-sook, and Sung-chul is the last boy, David. Chang-soo, then, is the second boy, Tommy. The Clarks' daughter wasn't first (clue 1), so she must be Yung-hee. The Doyle child isn't first either (clue 6); their child is second, and the Danielses' by elimination, first. By the same clue, then, Harry is Mr. Daniels. Jean's child, who isn't Molly, followed Jack's (clue 4), who's a boy (clue 2). Jean's child, then, must be Joy and her father Frank Clark. Molly, then, is the first child. Also by clue 4, Jack's is the second child, Tommy. By clue 2, Dottie has one of the new sons but isn't married to Jack; she's married to Bill and they have the fourth child. Linda, by elimination, is Jack Doyle's wife. In sum, in order of exiting children:

> Molly Mee-sook, Harry and Gail Daniels
> Tommy Chang-soo, Jack and Linda Doyle
> Joy Yung-hee, Frank and Jean Clark
> David Sung-chul, Bill and Dottie Potter

9. ANIMAL WELFARE

Of the five youngsters, one lost a dog and one found a dog (clue 1), Vic lost a cat (clue 2), one found a gray cat (clue 3), and one adopted a dog (clue 4). From clues 3 and 5, the Otis child must be Vic, while Irene found the gray cat. The adopted dog was not white, tan (clue 4), or spotted (clue 6); it was black. By clue 8, then, Vic Otis lost his white cat. The last name of the child who adopted the dog is not Hall (clue 6), Kent, or Macy (clue 10); it is Pate. The Kent child is then Irene (clue 1). The Macy child did not find a dog (clue 9) and must have lost one, while the Hall child found a dog. The latter was not spotted (clue 6), so it was tan, and the lost dog was spotted. The Hall child is not Eve (clue 6) or Joe (clue 7); he is Roy. Joe didn't adopt a dog (clue 7), so Eve did and Joe lost his dog. In sum:

> Roy Hall found the tan dog
> Irene Kent found the gray cat
> Joe Macy lost his spotted dog
> Vic Otis lost his white cat
> Eve Pate adopted a black dog

10.   FAVORITE PUZZLES

By clue 3, the five solvers are: Easterner Alma, Easterner Penny, the one who requested Word Arithmetics, the one who requested Cross Sums, and Quinn. The third Easterner is a man (clue 8), so Enid is from the West. Mike is from the West (introduction), so Vic is the man from the East. By clues 3 and 5, Vic requested either more Word Arithmetics or more Cross Sums. Quinn, who is not Alma, Penny, or Vic (clue 3), must be from the West Coast. Smith, then, is also from the West Coast (clue 2). Jones, Klein, and Cole are then the three from the East Coast and Penny must be Klein (clue 4). Vic is not Jones (clue 1), so Alma is, and Vic is Cole. An Easterner requested diagramlesses, but it was neither Vic nor Alma Jones (clue 1); Penny Klein requested them. Alma Jones did not request Word Arithmetics or Cross Sums (clue 3), or Logic Problems (clue 6), she requested Anacrostics. Quinn did not request Word Arithmetics or Cross Sums (clue 3), so Quinn's request was for Logic Problems. Quinn is therefore not Enid (clue 7), he is Mike and Enid is Smith. She did not request Word Arithmetics (clue 7), so she requested Cross Sums, and Vic Cole requested Word Arithmetics. In summary:

Vic Cole, Word Arithmetics
Penny Klein, Diagramlesses
Alma Jones, Anacrostics
Mike Quinn, Logic Problems
Enid Smith, Cross Sums

11.   A FRUITFUL EXPERIENCE

There were only four fruits used and each girl used a different combination of three (introduction and clue 1). The four possible different combinations are: 1) apples, cherries and grapes; 2) apples, cherries and bananas; 3) apples, bananas and grapes; and 4) bananas, cherries and grapes. Mandy and the Miller girl both used apples and cherries (clue 5). Robin is a third girl who used apples (clue 2), so she could not have used cherries, and must have used bananas and grapes. Erica isn't Miller (clue 4), so she is the fourth girl, and could not have used apples; she used bananas, cherries and grapes. By elimination, Staci is the Miller girl. Erica isn't the Clark girl (clue 4), and since we have already ascertained that Robin did not use cherries, she cannot be the Clark girl (clue 3); the Clark girl can only be Mandy, and she used apples, cherries and grapes. By elimination, Staci Miller used apples, cherries and bananas. The Flure girl didn't use both cherries and grapes (clue 3), so Robin must be the Flure girl, and Erica is the Jacobs girl. In sum:

Mandy Clark: apples, cherries, grapes
Robin Flure: apples, bananas, grapes
Erica Jacobs: bananas, cherries, grapes
Staci Miller: apples, cherries, bananas

12.   THE FOUR FRIENDS

Since Rob can't live in West Garden (clue 3), Terry doesn't live in North Garden (also clue 3). Terry can't live in South Garden (clue 1), so Rob doesn't live in East Garden (clue 3). If Rob lives in South Garden, then Terry lives in West Garden, which leaves no place West of Rob (clue 3) for Dale to live. Therefore, Rob lives in North Garden and Terry in East Garden. Betsy must live in South Garden (clue 1) and Dale by elimination lives in West Garden. Before Betsy and Terry moved last June, Terry lived in South Garden and Betsy in East Garden (clue 1). By clue 2, then, Dale's area of residence is the same now as it was before. Hence, so is Rob's. In sum, with the residential area before last June first, and the present one second:

Betsy: East Garden, South Garden
Dale: West Garden, West Garden
Rob: North Garden, North Garden
Terry: South Garden, East Garden

13. TWINS

The twins with the same sounding names are not the Gardners, Hamptons (clue 1), Irvings, or Johnsons (clue 5); they are the Kirkmans. Since all five are listed in clue 3, and Bobby and Bobbie are not brother and sister (also clue 3), by elimination, Gene (and his sister Jean) must be the Kirkmans and Bobby and Bobbie must be a Gardner and an Irving in one order or the other. The Gardner girl (who has the same sounding name as the Hampton boy—clue 1) cannot be Bobbie (clue 3); therefore Bobby must be Gardner and Bobbie's last name then is Irving. The Irving boy is neither Jerry nor Lew (clue 2); he is Gale. The Gardner girl cannot be Gail (clue 1), nor is she Lou (clue 4); she is Geri. The Hampton boy, then, is also Jerry (clue 1). By elimination, the Johnson boy is Lew. His sister is not Lou (clue 5); she is Gail. Lou is Jerry's sister. In summary:

> Bobby and Geri Gardner
> Jerry and Lou Hampton
> Gale and Bobbie Irving
> Lew and Gail Johnson
> Gene and Jean Kirkman

14. QUICK CLEAN-UP

By clue 2, Mandy, Mike, and Matt were the three oldest children. Since the youngest is a boy (clue 4), he must be Mack and the second youngest Molly. By clue 6, there is a child between Molly and Mike in age. Since the oldest is a boy (clue 4), the middle child must be Mandy. Therefore, the children from oldest to youngest must be Matt, Mike, Mandy, Molly, and Mack. Molly, then, hid the snack dishes (clue 1) and Mandy hid the comic books (clue 3). Since neither Matt nor Mack hid the toy cars (clue 4), Mike did. Matt didn't hide the baseball glove (clue 2); Mack did and Matt, by elimination, hid the Sunday paper. Mack didn't hide the glove in the T.V. cabinet (clue 2), nor did Matt, Mandy, or Mike hide anything in it; Molly did. Since a child older than Mandy put something under the sofa (clue 3), that leaves out Mack. Neither Mike nor Mandy hid anything under the sofa (clue 6); so Matt did. Mack didn't hide the baseball glove in the piano bench (clue 4) or under the chair (clue 5); he hid it, by elimination, behind the pillow. By clue 4, the toy cars Mike hid didn't go in the piano bench, so they must have gone under the chair and the comic books into the bench. In sum, from oldest to youngest:

> Matt: Sunday paper, sofa
> Mike: toy cars, chair
> Mandy: comic books, piano bench
> Molly: snack dishes, T.V. cabinet
> Mack: baseball glove, pillow

15. WORKING AT IT

By clue 1, the five couples are Tara and her husband; the Lewises; the veterinarian and her husband; the broker and his wife, Liza; and John Callus and his wife. Since John's wife isn't Dora or Kate, she is Mary. Dora, who isn't Mrs. Lewis (clue 5), can only be the veterinarian, and Mrs. Lewis is Kate. Mr. Davis the bartender isn't Dora's husband (clue 6), so his wife is Tara. Since Dora isn't married to Dave Collins (clue 5), Dave is Liza's husband. Dora and her husband, by elimination, are the McKays. Kate Lewis is a designer (clue 5). The physician and her husband the lawyer (clue 4) can only be Mary and John Callus. The secretary isn't Kate's husband (clue 5) and must be Dora's. Earl and his wife the nurse (clue 3) must be the Davises. Mr. Lewis must be the hotel manager mentioned in clue 2 and Tony is Mr. McKay. By elimination, Mr. Lewis' first name is Simon, and Liza is a dancer. In sum:

> Callus: physician Mary and lawyer John
> Collins: dancer Liza and broker Dave
> Davis: nurse Tara and bartender Earl
> Lewis: designer Kate and hotel manager Simon
> McKay: veterinarian Dora and secretary Tony

16.   SUNDAY BRUNCH

One couple is John Curtis, the father (clue 1), and Mary Curtis, his wife (clue 5). Mike and Nancy are a second couple (clue 3). Since no one sat next to his or her spouse (clue 2), Jack is not married to Tina (clue 4); he is married to Ellen. By elimination, Steve is married to Tina. Men and women alternated around the table (clue 2), with John Curtis at the head (clue 1). Since the three people on each side of the table had different last names (clue 6), Mrs. Curtis and her son did not sit on the same side; by clue 5, Mary Curtis sat around a corner from her son. Her son, then, sat at the foot of the table opposite his father, and Mary Curtis sat at his right (clue 5). Jack then sat on the side opposite Mary, between Tina and Mrs. Duncan (clue 4), and his last name is Bentley (clue 6). By clue 6, then, Tina's last name is Curtis; her spouse Steve is the Curtis son. Since Tina cannot sit next to her husband at the foot of the table, she sits at Jack's left, with Mrs. Duncan sitting at his right. By elimination, Mike and Nancy are the Duncans. Mike Duncan sat opposite Jack Bentley (clue 2) and, by elimination, Ellen Bentley sat between Mike and John Curtis. In summary, going clockwise around the table:

> John Curtis, Ellen Bentley, Mike Duncan, Mary Curtis,
> Steve Curtis, Nancy Duncan, Jack Bentley, and Tina Curtis.

17.   STARSHIP RIDE

By clue 3, the starships held boys and girls alternately. Since there were six starships evenly spaced, the ships opposite one another held a boy in one and a girl in the other. A girl was in each of the blue (clue 1), black (clue 4), and orange (clue 6) starships and a boy in each of the remaining yellow, red, and green ones. Girls were also in the "Fireball" (clue 1), "Hornet" (clue 4), and "Comet" (clue 5). The boys, then, were in the "Bullet," "Lightning," and "Blazer." The "Hornet" isn't black (clue 4) or blue (clue 7); it's orange. By clue 1, the "Fireball" isn't blue; it's black and the "Comet" is blue. Since by clue 1, Bob was behind the blue "Comet" and ahead of the black "Fireball," he must be opposite the girl in the orange "Hornet." By clue 4, Holly must be in the blue "Comet" ahead of Bob and opposite the "Blazer." Neither Dan (clue 6) nor Bob is in the "Blazer," so Mark is and Dan is in the starship ahead of Holly's. The "Lightning" isn't opposite the "Hornet" (clue 7) so it's not Bob's but Dan's. Bob, by elimination, is in the "Bullet." Also by clue 7, the "Lightning" isn't next to Gina's; so Gina must be opposite Dan in the "Fireball," and Lisa, by elimination, in the "Hornet." Neither Dan's starship nor the "Blazer" is red (clue 6), so Bob's is. By clue 2, Dan's starship behind Lisa's isn't yellow; it's green and Mark's "Blazer" yellow. In sum clockwise:

> Bob, red "Bullet"
> Holly, blue "Comet"
> Dan, green "Lightning"
> Lisa, orange "Hornet"
> Mark, yellow "Blazer"
> Gina, black "Fireball"

18.   THE THANKSGIVING PAGEANT

From the introduction, we know each grade was represented by one boy and one girl. Each grade had one people role (Indian or Pilgrim) and one food role (clue 8); the fourth-grade people role was a Pilgrim (clue 6). Karen, who played an Indian, was a grade above Dave (clue 1), and was also older than Bob, who played the other Indian (clue 5). So Karen was in the third grade; Dave was then in the second grade; Bob must have been a first-grader. The second-grade people role must have been that of the other Pilgrim. By clue 4, John and Anne, who represented the same grade, can only have been the fourth-graders. Tina played one of the Pilgrims, her brother the other one (clue 3); John must be Tina's brother who played the fourth-grade Pilgrim (clue 6), while Anne played the ear of corn (clue 4). Tina was then the second-grade Pilgrim, and her classmate, Dave, played the turkey (clue 2). Steve, who played a pumpkin (clue 7), must have been the third-grade boy. By elimination, the first-grade girl was Ellen and she dressed as a cranberry. In sum:

1st grade: Bob, Indian; Ellen, cranberry
2nd grade: Tina, Pilgrim; Dave, turkey
3rd grade: Karen, Indian; Steve, pumpkin
4th grade: John, Pilgrim; Anne, corn

19. MOVING DAY

Four of the five families are Robert, who moved from a condo (clue 1), the Bentleys, who moved to a condo (clue 1), a widow, who moved from a house to an apartment (clue 2), and a married couple, who moved from an apartment to a house (clue 2). The widow has a daughter (clue 2), so is not Sarah (clue 3), nor Lois or Karen (clue 5). She is Madeline. John's wife is not Lois or Karen (clue 5), so she is Sarah. David's wife is not Karen (clue 6), so is Lois; Steve's wife (clue 4), by elimination, is Karen. The only man without a wife is Robert, so he must be bachelor Fisher who moved into an apartment (clue 7). Madeline's daughter and son-in-law, who moved from an apartment to Madeline's house (clue 2), are not Sarah and John (clue 3), nor Steve and Karen (clue 4), so must be David and Lois. Widow Madeline's last name is not Madison (clues 2, 6). By clue 6, the Madisons are not David and Lois, so the Madisons are the fifth family and they moved from an apartment. They are not Sarah and John (clue 3), so must be Steve and Karen. They didn't move into a house (clue 4), so they moved to a condo. Sarah and John, by elimination, are the Bentleys, who didn't move from an apartment (clue 3); they moved from a house. Madeline is not Hunter (clue 8), so she is Swanson; David and Lois, by elimination, are the Hunters. In summary:

John and Sarah Bentley, house to condo
Robert Fisher, condo to apartment
David and Lois Hunter, apartment to house
Steve and Karen Madison, apartment to condo
Madeline Swanson, house to apartment

20. BOWLING TEAM DINNER

Each order was different (clue 1), meaning that three of the men had antipasto, each with a different one of the three possible entrees, and the other three had minestrone, again each with a different entree. Clue 2, which mentions all six men, must mean that Bob, King, and a man who ordered ravioli all had the same first course but three different entrees; while Chuck, Hall, and a man who ordered spaghetti had the other first course and three different entrees. Hall didn't have lasagna (clue 3), so he must have had ravioli and Chuck lasagna. Also by clue 3, Chuck is White and Gary, who also had lasagna, must have had the other first course and can only be King. Bob, by elimination, had spaghetti. Neither Frank nor Pinza had ravioli (clue 4), so they are the two who had spaghetti and Bob's last name is Pinza, while Frank is the unnamed man mentioned in clue 2 who had the same first course as Chuck White and Hall. That wasn't minestrone (also clue 4), so it was antipasto. Bob Pinza and Gary King must both have had minestrone. By clue 5, Veery, who isn't Frank, must be the man who had minestrone and ravioli; since he isn't Ed, Hall is. By elimination, Frank's surname is Noyes, and Veery's first name is Dave. In sum,

antipasto: Ed Hall, ravioli
Frank Noyes, spaghetti
Chuck White, lasagna
minestrone: Gary King, lasagna
Bob Pinza, spaghetti
Dave Veery, ravioli

21. THE PAINT WAS FREE

According to clue 2 the five couples are: the Golds; the two couples who bought solid-color carpet; the couple who bought a patterned carpet; and the couple who chose gold paint. Two couples bought tweed carpet (clue 3). One of the tweed-carpet buyers was the Greens (clue 3), so the other tweed-carpet buyer, by elimination in clue 2, is the Golds, and they chose blue paint (clue 3). The Greens, then, must be the fifth couple in clue 2 who chose gold paint. The Whites chose the same color paint as the Browns' carpet (clue 4), which could not be brown or white (clue 1); so the Whites chose green paint. The Browns' carpet is then green (clue 4). The Browns didn't choose the brown paint (clue 1), so they chose white paint and the Blacks, by elimination, chose the brown paint. The Whites' carpet was then brown (clue 4). The two couples who chose paint the same color as their carpets (clue 5) were not the Whites, Blacks, or Browns. They were the Golds, who chose blue carpet to match their blue paint, and the Greens, who chose gold carpet to match their gold paint. The Blacks, then, bought the white carpet. The Browns' green carpet was not solid (clue 6), so it was patterned, and the Whites' brown carpet and the Blacks' white carpet were the two solid-color carpets. In summary:

> Blacks, white solid carpet, brown paint
> Browns, green patterned carpet, white paint
> Golds, blue tweed carpet, blue paint
> Greens, gold tweed carpet, gold paint
> Whites, brown solid carpet, green paint

22.   FOOTBALL TICKETS

In the exchanges of seats, all the men and only the men were involved: Joe moved from Row K to Row J, trading seats with Ed (clue 3), and Sandra's husband moved from Row J to Row K, trading seats with Mary's husband (clue 4). By clue 1, then, Gus, who was in seat J-116, is Sandra's husband, she was in seat K-116, and he moved to seat K-117 to sit beside her. Mary's husband was then in seat K-117 and moved to seat J-116, so Mary's seat was J-117. By clue 2, Diane's seat was K-119, and her husband's was J-119; he must be Ed, and he moved to seat K-118 to sit beside Diane. Joe then moved from seat K-118 to seat J-119, so his wife's seat was J-118. By elimination, Mary's husband is Bob and Joe's wife is Beth. In sum:

> Beth (J-118) & Joe (K-118 to J-119)
> Diane (K-119) & Ed (J-119 to K-118)
> Mary (J-117) & Bob (K-117 to J-116)
> Sandra (K-116) & Gus (J-116 to K-117)

23.   THE MANSIONS

We are told that each of the four mansions has two or more of these three extras: sauna, swimming pool, tennis court. By clue 1, we know that no two of the four families have the same combination of these three luxury items. Therefore, one mansion has a sauna and a swimming pool, a second a sauna and a tennis court, a third a swimming pool and a tennis court, and the fourth all three items. We note from this that each of the three luxuries is owned by three families. By clue 5, the Newells live at either #2 or #8 and have a swimming pool. Suppose they live at #2. Then two other families have pools, and they live at #'s 4 and 6 (clue 4). The family at #8 would be the one with a tennis court and a sauna, so they could not be the Parrs (clue 3). The O'Briens can't live at #8 because then the Parrs and the Quincys would be in #4 or #6 in one order or the other, contradicting clue 3. So #8 would have to be occupied by the Quincys (clue 3), while the Parrs would live at #4. By elimination, the O'Briens would live at #6. By clue 6, they would be the one with all three extras. But this would contradict clue 2. Therefore, the Newells live at #8 rather than #2, and the other two families with pools live at #'s 4 and 6 (clue 4). The family living at #2 has a sauna and a tennis court, so are not the Parrs; they are the Quincys, and the Parrs live at #6. By clue 3, the Parrs have a tennis court as well as a swimming pool. By elimination, the O'Briens live at #4, and by clue 6, have all three extras. The Newells then have a pool and a sauna. In sum:

> #2: Quincy (sauna and tennis court)
> #4: O'Brien (sauna, swimming pool, tennis court)
> #6: Parr (swimming pool, tennis court)
> #8: Newell (sauna, swimming pool)

24. GRANDMA PERKINS' GIFTS

By clue 3, Ben was nine in September, and he has exactly two sisters, one ten and the other twelve. Thirteen-year-old Jane (clue 4) is therefore his cousin. No two siblings were born in the same month (introduction), so fourteen-year-old Jon, whose birthday is in September, and his sister Adele (clue 1) cannot be Ben's siblings and must be Jane's. Since Ben has two sisters (clue 3) and there are only two girls left, Candy and Elenita must be Ben's sisters. Candy's and Donald's birthdays are both in October (clue 2), so they are not siblings. So, Donald is Jane's, Jon's, and Adele's brother, and they are the four Sweeneys, while Ben and his sisters are the Perkins children. Since all the children are different ages (introduction), and Jane is thirteen (clue 4), by clue 6, Donald can only have turned eleven on his last birthday, while Candy is the ten-year-old. The twelve-year-old, in clue 3, is Elenita; her birthday is in November, as is Jane's (clue 2). Again since siblings were born in different months, Adele's birthday is in December; she received eight dollars (clue 5). In sum:

> Ben Perkins: September, $9
> Candy Perkins: October, $10
> Elenita Perkins: November, $12
> Jon Sweeney: September, $14
> Donald Sweeney: October, $11
> Jane Sweeney: November, $13
> Adele Sweeney: December, $8

25. SPECIALTY CAMPS

By clue 8, Audrey spoke before the girl who told about the tennis camp, who spoke right before the one who had gone to camp in Maine. Audrey did not go to the sailing camp (clue 6), nor is that camp in Maine (clue 4), so the one who went to sailing camp is the fourth girl. The one who went to camp in Maine isn't Dora (clue 4) nor, since the tennis-camp speaker spoke just before the Maine camp speaker, is it Carol (clue 5), so she is Bess. That camp isn't the music camp (clue 3), the tennis camp (clue 8) or the sailing camp (clue 4), so it specializes in riding, and the music camp is Audrey's. Carol spoke after Bess (clue 5) and must be the one who went to sailing camp, while the one who went to the tennis camp is Dora. By clue 2, Audrey's last name is Thomas, and Dora's camp is in New York. Audrey's camp is not in Ohio (clue 1), so Carol's is, and Audrey's is in Michigan. The Rogers girl is not Bess (clue 3) or Carol (clue 7); she is Dora. Carol is not the Strong girl (clue 5), so Bess is, and Carol's last name, by elimination, is Unger. In sum, in order of their speeches:

> Audrey Thomas: music, Mich.
> Dora Rogers: tennis, N.Y.
> Bess Strong: riding, Me.
> Carol Unger: sailing, Ohio

26. DEDICATED TO THE ONES I LOVE

Dan is three years older than the child to whom *Fritz's Fantasy* was dedicated (clue 2), who is nine years older than Nan, who is at least two years old (clue 5). Dan, then, must be between fourteen and eighteen, *Fritz's Fantasy*'s child between eleven and fifteen, and Nan between two and six. By clue 1, Ann can only be four, eight, twelve, or sixteen years old, Van is two, four, six, or eight years old, and the child to whom *Private Puzzle* was dedicated is one through four years old. Since there is a nine-year-old (clue 4), clues 1, 2, and 5 must overlap by two children. The only possibility is that Ann is the child to whom *Fritz's Fantasy* was dedicated and she is 12 years old. Dan, then is fifteen, Van six, and Nan, to whom *Private Puzzle* was dedicated, is three. By elimination, Jan is the nine-year-old. *Worried Willy* must have been dedicated to Van (clue 3). *The Carlton Charade* was, then, dedicated to Dan (clue 4), and *The Millstone Mystery* to Jan. In summary:

> Dan, 15, *The Carlton Charade*
> Ann, 12, *Fritz's Fantasy*

27. ANCESTRAL JOURNEYS

Carl, an engineer, was scheduled to depart on Thursday (clue 6). Two of the travelers were scheduled to depart on the weekend (clue 1), i.e., Saturday and Sunday. We know that one traveler was leaving the same day, Monday. The nurse's departure was one day before the trip to Lisbon, and neither was on the weekend (clue 2); the doctor left still earlier in the week (clue 3). Therefore Carl, the engineer, was headed for Lisbon on Thursday, the nurse's departure was Wednesday, and the doctor's was Monday. The writer's trip to Canton wasn't starting on Sunday (clue 4), so that departure was Saturday and the lawyer's Sunday. The nurse is a woman (clue 2), and the two leaving on the weekend were George and Bryant (clue 1) so Gary Young (clue 7) can only be the doctor. Tim, whose destination was Dublin (clue 5), can only be the lawyer, and his last name must be Bryant; George, then, is the writer. The nurse, by elimination, is Maria. Gary's destination wasn't Manila (clue 7), so it was Tokyo and Maria's was Manila. Jansen, a man, departed after Burns, but not last (clue 8) so they are respectively Carl and Maria. George's last name, by elimination, is Lee. In sum:

Monday: Dr. Gary Young, Tokyo
Wednesday: nurse Maria Burns, Manila
Thursday: engineer Carl Jansen, Lisbon
Saturday: writer George Lee, Canton
Sunday: lawyer Tim Bryant, Dublin

28. SWEET-TOOTH SATISFACTION

By clue 6, these three guests selected candies consecutively: the one who took the chocolate-filled piece, Davis, and Tara. The clue also tells us that the chocolate-filled piece was not third, so the selections were not the third, fourth, and fifth. If they were the second, third, and fourth, then the fourth candy, Tara's, would have been mint-filled (clue 2), which would contradict clue 4. Therefore, the chocolate-filled piece was the first taken, Davis's choice was second, and Tara's was third. The mint-filled candy was the fourth taken, and Ms. Olson made the last choice (clue 2). Neither Ms. Olson (clue 2) nor Tara (clue 4) had the candy with the coconut filling, so Davis did. By clue 3, Tara must be the one who had the candy with vanilla filling and Ms. Olson's candy, by elimination, had caramel filling. By clue 1, the chocolate- and caramel-filled candies were dark chocolate, and all the rest were milk chocolate. By clue 5, since Mary's candy was milk chocolate but Larsen didn't take the vanilla-filled candy, Mary must be Davis and Larsen must have taken the first piece of candy. Since Olson is a Ms., by elimination, she is Lynn. By clue 7, Andy can only be Larsen, Bill took the fourth piece of candy, and Baker is Tara's last name. Bill's surname, by elimination, is Tyler. In sum, in chronological order:

Andy Larsen: chocolate, dark
Mary Davis: coconut, milk
Tara Baker: vanilla, milk
Bill Tyler: mint, milk
Lynn Olson: caramel, dark

29. SHIPMATES

By clues 3 and 6, the supply officer is Hugh. By clue 4, Ensign Bulkhead is the personnel officer who must have served on the *Phantom* (clue 3). By elimination in clue 3, Ensign Briggs is the munitions officer. By substitution in clue 1, therefore, Ensign Bulkhead, who served on the *Phantom,* must be Will and Briggs served on the *Steve Canyon;* by elimination in clue 1, Hugh is Ensign Bridges. Hugh did not serve on the *Steve Roper* (clue 2) or the *Charlie Brown* (clue 7), so he served on the *Prince Valiant.* Again by clue 2, Vic is not

148

munitions officer Briggs who served on the *Steve Canyon* and did not serve on the *Steve Roper* (also clue 2), so he served on the *Charlie Brown*. Stan didn't serve on the *Steve Roper* (clue 8), so Ted did and Stan served on the *Steve Canyon* and is therefore Ensign Briggs. The communications officer can't be Ted who served on the *Steve Roper* (clue 8), so he is Vic; Ted, by elimination, is recreation officer. Ted is not Ensign Stern (clue 5), so Vic is, and Ted is Ensign Forward. In sum, the ensigns' full names, their first duty ships, and their responsibilities on the *Dick Tracy* are:

Hugh Bridges	*Prince Valiant*	supply
Stan Briggs	*Steve Canyon*	munitions
Will Bulkhead	*Phantom*	personnel
Ted Forward	*Steve Roper*	recreation
Vic Stern	*Charlie Brown*	communications

30. I LOVE YOU

One boy and one girl live on each street (clue 1). The boys are: Matt on Oak Street (clue 2), the Douglas boy on Ash Street (clue 4), Chuck on Maple Street (clue 6), and the Putnam boy on Elm Street (clue 8). The girls are: the Walker girl on Oak Street (clue 2), Jean on Ash Street (clue 4), the Manning girl on Maple Street (clue 6), and Wendy on Elm Street (clue 8). Roger is not the Putnam boy (clue 3), so he is the Douglas child and, by elimination, Putnam's first name is Dave. Dave Putnam sent his card to the Clayborne girl, who sent hers to Matt (clue 7). Dave received one from the Manning girl, who received one from Roger Douglas (clue 3). These five are thus: Roger Douglas on Ash Street sent one to Miss Manning on Maple Street, who sent one to Dave Putnam on Elm Street, who sent one to Miss Clayborne, who sent one to Matt on Oak Street. Miss Clayborne, who received a valentine from Dave Putnam on Elm Street, is not Wendy from Elm Street (clue 1), so she is Jean from Ash Street. Matt from Oak Street did not send one to Miss Walker on Oak Street (clue 1), so he sent his to Wendy on Elm Street. By elimination, Wendy sent hers to Chuck on Maple Street, who sent his to Miss Walker on Oak Street. Roger Douglas did not send his card to Pam (clue 5), so Pam is Miss Walker. Chuck is then the Baxter child (clue 5). Matt's last name is Johnson and Wendy is Rockwell (clue 9). By elimination, Miss Manning is Barbara. In summary:

Barbara Manning on Maple sent to
Dave Putnam on Elm, who sent to
Jean Clayborne on Ash, who sent to
Matt Johnson on Oak, who sent to
Wendy Rockwell on Elm, who sent to
Chuck Baxter on Maple, who sent to
Pam Walker on Oak, who sent to
Roger Douglas on Ash, who sent to
Barbara

31. RENDEZVOUS IN MARSEILLES

We know each agent traveled part way by either train or plane and that his other mode of travel differed from that of the other agents; no two of the travel combinations, therefore, were the same. One agent started his trip by train and finished on a bicycle (clues 1, 7). A second agent started by train and finished by motorcycle (clue 4). A third, the Englishman, started by plane and finished in a car (clue 8). A fourth, Horace, started by bus (clue 3). A fifth, the Spaniard, started on horseback (clue 2). The sixth, Raoul, traveled by ship and plane, in one order or the other (clue 9). The Greek who arrived by train (clue 5) can only be Horace; Philip, the only agent to arrive by plane (clue 6), can only be the Spaniard. Raoul then took the plane first and finished by ship. By clue 2, Donald must be the Englishman. Carl is not the bicyclist (clue 7) and must be the one who arrived by motorcycle; the bicyclist, by elimination, is the Frenchman, Pierre. By clue 4, Carl is not the American, so Raoul is, and Carl, by elimination, is the Italian. In sum, with the modes of travel in chronological order:

Carl, Italy: train, motorcycle
Donald, England: plane, car
Horace, Greece: bus, train
Philip, Spain: horseback, plane
Pierre, France: train, bicycle
Raoul, U.S.A.: plane, ship

32. WORD POWER

There are two boys, Bob and Ray. By clue 3, a sixth-grade boy, who wasn't Bob and must
therefore have been Ray, offered a definition of *gerbera*. Eva is also a sixth-grader (clue 5).
By clue 2, a seventh-grade girl, who wasn't Beth and must have been Lucy offered "English
coin" as a definition. A fourth child, neither Eva nor Lucy, tried to define *eidolon* (clue 4).
Lucy didn't try to define *dichotomy* or *widgeon* (clue 2), so her word was *quidnunc*. The
child who offered "sermon" as a definition wasn't Ray (clue 1)—but that child was a boy
(clue 6), so he was Bob; since he didn't attempt to define *eidolon* (also clue 6), he is the fifth
child. The one who tried to define *eidolon*, by elimination, was Beth. The seventh-grader
who offered "medicine" as a definition (clue 7), can only have been Beth. Bob is also a
seventh-grader (clue 8). Eva didn't try to define *dichotomy* (clue 1), so Bob did. Ray's
definition of *gerbera* wasn't "gadget" (clue 3), so that was Eva's definition. By elimination,
Ray's definition was "grouch," and Eva tried to define *widgeon*. In sum:

> Beth, 7th: *eidolon*, "medicine"
> Bob, 7th: *dichotomy*, "sermon"
> Eva, 6th: *widgeon*, "gadget"
> Lucy, 7th: *quidnunc*, "English coin"
> Ray, 6th: *gerbera*, "grouch"

33. GLADYS GROWS GLADS

We are told that no woman grows flowers with the same name as her own. The woman who
grows lilies lives at number 208 (clue 4). By clue 8, no woman grows flowers with the same
name as her next-door neighbor. Therefore, Lily cannot live at 206 or 210; nor does she live
at 204 (clue 1), so Lily lives at 212. Ms. Black, who lives at either 206 or 208 (clue 3), is not
Lily or Rose (also clue 3); nor is she Dahlia or Violet (clue 7), so she is Daisy. By clue 1, the
woman who grows daisies must live at either 206 or 210. If she lived at 206, Daisy Black
could not live at either 206 or 208 (clue 8), so the daisies grow at 210 and Daisy Black lives at
206. By clue 2, the woman who grows roses must live at 204; by clue 6, she is Ms. Green.
Now, by clue 1, Ms. Brown lives at 208. By clue 5, Ms. Gray lives at 212 and Ms. White at
210. Lily Gray does not grow violets, (clue 5), so Daisy Black does, and Lily, by elimination,
grows dahlias. Therefore, by clue 8 again, Violet lives at 210. Since Rose can't be the rose
grower, she is Ms. Brown, and Ms. Green is Dahlia. In sum:

> 204: Dahlia Green, roses
> 206: Daisy Black, violets
> 208: Rose Brown, lilies
> 210: Violet White, daisies
> 212: Lily Gray, dahlias

34. THE EXPLORERS QUIZ

Since all three were wrong about the discovery mentioned in clue 2, it was not the
Mississippi, the Pacific, or Florida. Nor was it Peru (clue 5), so it was Mexico. Since all the
children picked the same discoverer in clue 4, he was then none of those mentioned in clue
2, and, again, since all three were wrong, he was not Pizarro; he was Cortez. Each child was
right on exactly one pairing (clue 1). Based on what has been established thus far, neither
John nor Andy was correct about De Soto's Mississippi, so that was Sally's correct answer.
Her other answers must have been that Balboa discovered Florida and Pizarro the Pacific.

Both Andy's and John's right answers were about either De Leon or Pizarro. If Andy had been right about De Leon, then he would also have paired Pizarro with Peru as well (since Sally paired Pizarro with the Pacific and by clue 3, no two agreed)—contradicting clue 1. So Andy correctly paired only Pizarro and Peru, and John was right about De Leon's discovery of Florida. The remaining wrong answers, by elimination: Andy paired De Soto with Florida and De Leon with the Pacific; John matched Balboa with Peru and Pizarro with the Mississippi. In sum, with the correct answers in capitals:

	Andy	*John*	*Sally*
Balboa	Mexico	Peru	Florida
Cortez	Mississippi	Pacific	Peru
De Leon	Pacific	FLORIDA	Mexico
De Soto	Florida	Mexico	MISSISSIPPI
Pizarro	PERU	Mississippi	Pacific

35. THE SCHOONER'S CREW

We have been told that the first crew member was signed on four years ago. Joe, who speaks Malay, has served for one year and was the last crew member to be hired (clue 3). By clue 5, then, the four-year man was hired in Hong Kong, Kriss has served for two years, and Joe signed on in Saigon one year ago. The first hired was not Kim or Shark (clue 4), or Lum (clue 6), so he was Dirk. By clue 1, then, the crew member hired at Macao has served three years and the one hired at Manila has served two and a half. By clue 7, the only other crew member has served a year and a half. By clue 4, Kim signed on at Manila, and Shark is the one who has served eighteen months. By elimination, the one who signed on at Macao is Lum; he speaks Chinese (clue 6). The one who was hired at Singapore and speaks Portuguese is not Kriss (clue 2) so he is Shark. Kriss, by elimination, signed on at Davao. Dirk speaks neither Tagalog nor Moro (clue 8), so he speaks Spanish; Kim does not speak Moro (clue 1), so Kriss does and Kim speaks Tagalog. In sum, in order of length of service:

> 4 years.: Dirk, Hong Kong, Spanish
> 3 years.: Lum, Macao, Chinese
> 2½ yrs.: Kim, Manila, Tagalog
> 2 yrs.: Kriss, Davao, Moro
> 1½ yrs.: Shark, Singapore, Portuguese
> 1 yr.: Joe, Saigon, Malay

36. EIGHT KIDS AND ONE BATH

By the introduction and clue 3, the time from 6 to 6:15 is scheduled for one of the girls. By clue 5, an eight-year-old child is scheduled to begin use of the bath at 6:35. Since there are twenty minutes between 6:15 and 6:35, it follows that both the second and the third user of the bath are boys—the first scheduled for 6:15–6:25, the second for 6:25–6:35. By clue 2, Christopher is supposed to finish his time at 7, so he is scheduled to go in at 6:50, and the eight-year-old who precedes him is the fourth to use the bath, a girl with the scheduled time of 6:35–6:50. From clues 4 and 9, Darryl uses the bath just before Michelle, and Jim's time is later than Michelle's and just before the six-year-old's time. So Darryl and Michelle must be among the first four to use the bath. In order to fit into the time schedule already established with girl, boy, boy, girl, Darryl must be the third and Michelle the eight-year-old who is the fourth bathroom user. Jim isn't the last to use the bath (clue 9), and since Lois and Kate use the bath one after the other (clue 7), Jim must be the sixth, and Lois and Kate the seventh and eighth respectively. Lois, then, is the six-year-old who follows Jim (clue 9), and, Kate, then, is seven (clue 7). The times set for Jim, Lois, and Kate can only be 7–7:10, 7:10–7:25, and 7:25–7:40 respectively. By elimination, the first to use the bath is Holly and the second is Bill. Jim is 12 years old (clue 4); Holly is 11 (clue 6). Of Bill, Darryl, and Christopher, one is nine, another is 10, and the third is a twin, whose age we must determine. Bill isn't a twin (clue 1), and we know that the twins' time periods are consecutive (clue 8). If Darryl and Michelle were twins, then Darryl would be eight years old, and Christopher—since he is a year younger than Darryl (clue 1)—would be Kate's twin, a contradiction. Christopher is not the oldest (clue 1), so he can't be Jim's twin. By elimination, the twins must be Michelle and Christopher, who are both eight. Darryl, then, is nine and Bill is 10 (clue 1). In summary:

6:00–6:15: Holly, 11
6:15–6:25: Bill, 10
6:25–6:35: Darryl, 9
6:35–6:50: Michelle, 8
6:50–7:00: Christopher, 8
7:00–7:10: Jim, 12
7:10–7:25: Lois, 6
7:25–7:40: Kate, 7

37. THE RECITAL

By clue 1 "Summer" was performed either third or fourth. By clue 2, "Winter" was also performed either third or fourth, and Ralph was among the four who played first and second—as were Nancy (clue 3), and Karen (clue 4), and Melba (clue 5); the four who played third and fourth then included Hiram, Joyce, Oscar, and Tommy. By clues 2 and 3, pianist Dills performed immediately before Hiram and immediately before "Winter," so Hiram played "Winter." If "Summer" were third and "Winter" fourth, then Dills would have played "Summer" (clue 2), but that contradicts clue 8, so "Winter" was the third duet played, "Summer" fourth. Then, Dills played piano in the second duo, and Ralph was one of the first. Nancy played with Ralph (clue 3), and Karen and Melba played the second duet. Oscar didn't play "Summer" (clue 6) and must have played "Winter" with Hiram; "Summer" was then played by Joyce and Tommy. Pianist Dills isn't Melba (clue 8) and must be Karen, while Melba played violin with her. Quest isn't Oscar (clue 6), so by clue 4, Quest is Hiram. Oscar is then violinist Young (clue 1), so Hiram Quest is a pianist. Early is Melba (clue 7). By clue 9, Inman is the pianist who played last and isn't Nancy, Ralph, or Tommy; Inman can only be Joyce, and Tommy is "Summer's" violinist. Tommy is then Levin (clue 10). Finally, by clue 11, violinist Grant is Nancy, and it was Karen and Melba who played "Spring." By elimination, Ralph's last name is Upton, and he and Nancy performed "Autumn." In sum, in order of performance:

Title	Piano	Violin
"Autumn"	—Ralph Upton	& Nancy Grant
"Spring"	—Karen Dills	& Melba Early
"Winter"	—Hiram Quest	& Oscar Young
"Summer"	—Joyce Inman	& Tommy Levin

38. SUPER ATHLETES

Since the chart shows that 15 points were given out in every event, there were no ties in any event, and, in the completed chart, each column of scores will contain a 5, a 4, a 3, a 2, and a 1 (intro). The fourth girl listed in the chart got 9 points in total, so, in the freestyle swimming and pushups events together she made 6 points. Those six points did not come from winning 3 points in each of the two events, as this would score a duplication in a column which is impossible (intro), nor did they come from making 5 points in one event and 1 in the other (another duplication in the chart). So the fourth girl in the chart got 2 points in one of these two events and 4 points in the other. Liz got 6 points for the freestyle and dash events together (chart). She didn't achieve these 6 points by getting 3 points in each event (duplication in dash column of chart). By clue 4, she got the same score in two events, so didn't get the 6 points with a 2 in one event and a 4 in the other; she got them with a 1 in freestyle swimming and a 5 in the dash. By elimination, Marcie made either 2 or 4 points in the freestyle swimming event. By clue 1, she made either 2 points or 4 points in the pushups event, so Dunn made 1 point in that event. By clue 5, Newton got 4 points and Marcie 2 in the pushups event, and Newton is the fourth person in the chart. In order to add up to 9, Newton made 2 points in the freestyle event, and Marcie made 4 points. By clue 7, the chart, and the fact there were no ties in any event, Moore made 2 points in the 55-yard dash, and Kathleen's last name is Newton. By elimination, Dunn made 4 points in the dash event. Elena isn't Moore (clue 6), so must be Dunn. By elimination, Jane is Moore. She made more than 10 points in total, so the woman she tied, Ms. Finney (clue 2), can only be Marcie. By

152

elimination, Ms. Pauley is Liz. By clue 3 and the chart, Marcie must be the girl with two second-place finishes, so she made a 4 in basketball shooting, for a total of 13 points. Jane, then, made 3 points in the basketball shooting event (clue 2). By elimination, Elena made 5 points in basketball shooting, gaining 15 total points and the win. In summary:

First Name	Last Name	200-meter freestyle	55-yard dash	Pushups	Basket-ball throw	TOTAL
Elena	Dunn	5	4	1	5	15
Marcie	Finney	4	3	2	4	13
Jane	Moore	3	2	5	3	13
Kathleen	Newton	2	1	4	2	9
Liz	Pauley	1	5	3	1	10
TOTAL		15	15	15	15	60

39. TUG OF WAR

By clue 5, Al was at the head of Team A, face-to-face with the treasurer, who was at the head of Team B. There were at least four people to the right of Tom (clue 2), so he, like Al, was on Team A. The other two people on Team A were either Bea or Pam (clue 3) and either Sara or Dave (clue 4); by these same clues, Team B also included either Bea or Pam and either Sara or Dave. By elimination, the other two people on Team B were Cathy and Rob. By clue 1, Team B consisted of Cathy, Fox, the personnel manager, and the sales manager. Mr. Lentz, who was directly in front of the sales manager, can only be the personnel manager. There is no place on Team B for a Mr. Werr who is the accountant, so by clue 4, Sara was the last member of Team A; directly in front of her was Mr. Werr, the accountant; and Dave was on Team B, the last one on his end of the rope. Dave isn't the sales manager (clue 4) and since Mr. Lentz is in front of the sales manager (clue 1), Dave must be Mr. Fox. At this point, the order for Team B is: the treasurer; Mr. Lentz the personnel manager; the sales manager; and Dave Fox. Cathy can only be the treasurer, while Lentz is Rob. There is no place on Team B for Bea, the vice president (clue 3), so Pam is the sales manager on Team B, while Bea was on Team A, between Mr. Werr and Al; Tom must be Mr. Werr. Pam's surname is Brown (clue 2). Now, by clue 6, since the only person on Team B whose surname has not been established is Cathy, her last name must be Cane, and Dave is the file clerk, while Al's last name is Jones, and the secretary is Sara. Smith, who isn't Sara (clue 4), must be Bea. By elimination, Sara's last name is Young, and Al Jones is the company president. In sum:

Team A, left to right:
    Secretary Sara Young
    Accountant Tom Werr
    Vice president Bea Smith
    President Al Jones

Team B, left to right:
    Treasurer Cathy Cane
    Personnel manager Rob Lentz
    Sales manager Pam Brown
    File clerk Dave Fox

40. TELEPHONE TIE-UP

A girl called Rick (clue 1); a second call went to Brian (clue 2); since Tom didn't talk to Brian (also 2), his was a third call; the fourth call was between two girls who discussed French (clue 3). Neither Cathy (clue 3) nor Karen (clue 5) talked about French, so Holly and Patty did. Two boys had the shortest conversation (clue 4), and Tom wasn't one of them (clue 2); the shortest call must have been made to Brian by Tom's brother Joe. Remember

153

that all the calls were different lengths. Tom's call was twice as long as Joe's (clue 2), while Karen's was twice as long as that of the girls who discussed French (clue 5), so Karen isn't the girl Tom called. Karen must be the one who called Rick and Cathy must be the girl Tom called. We know Tom's call was twice as long as Joe's, the shortest, and Karen's call was twice as long as Holly's—and the lengths of all the calls together totaled sixty minutes. If Joe's had been ten minutes and Tom's twenty, then the other two would have had to be ten and twenty minutes. If Joe's had been fifteen minutes (and Tom's thirty), it could not have been the shortest. Joe's call therefore must have taken five minutes and Tom's ten, leaving forty-five minutes, so Karen's call took thirty minutes and Holly's fifteen. Neither Joe nor Karen called to talk about movies (clue 4), so Tom did. Karen didn't call to discuss basketball (clue 1), so Joe did, and Karen called about the party. In sum:

> Joe called Brian: basketball, 5 minutes
> Tom called Cathy: movies, 10 minutes
> Holly called Patty: French, 15 minutes
> Karen called Rick: party, 30 minutes

41. ALOHA GARDENS

By clues 1, 3, and 7, the owners of cottages #1, #2, and #4 planted flame trees, and by clues, 2, 3, and 4, Hubbard, Barnes, and Nelson planted plumerias. By elimination, they are the owners of #3, #5, and #6, in one order or another, and the owners of #1, #2, and #4 are, in one order or another, Cooper, Baker, and Saunders. The owner of #2, who planted an orange tree (clue 3), cannot be Cooper (clue 1), and as no owner planted two citrus (introduction), he cannot be Baker, who planted a lime and a cherry (clue 5), therefore he is Saunders. By clue 1, Cooper cannot be the owner of #4, so he owns #1, and Baker, by elimination, owns #4. The owner of #3 can't be Nelson (clue 4) and, since #3 has a planted papaya, Hubbard, who didn't plant a papaya (clue 2) doesn't own #3; Barnes does. By clue 3, Barnes also planted a banana, so he is the only one who didn't plant a citrus. In other words, each of the other owners must have planted at least one citrus tree (intro). Therefore, since the owner of #5 planted a litchi, he could not be Hubbard, who planted a pomegranate (clue 2), the owner of #5 is Nelson. The owner of #6, by elimination, is Hubbard. By clue 7, the owner of #1 planted an avocado. As he did not plant the grapefruit or tangerine he must have planted the lemon, and as Nelson did not plant the grapefruit (clue 4) he must have planted the tangerine, and Hubbard, therefore, the grapefruit. Saunders, by elimination, planted the mango. In sum:

> Baker, #4, flame, lime, cherry
> Barnes #3, plumeria, banana, papaya
> Cooper, #1, flame, lemon, avocado
> Hubbard, #6, plumeria, grapefruit, pomegranate
> Nelson, #5, plumeria, tangerine, litchi
> Saunders, #2, flame, orange, mango

42. GIFT SUBSCRIPTIONS

We are told that the five subscriptions together will bring George 100 additional magazines a year, and that at least one is published monthly, accounting for twelve copies. One is weekly, with 52 copies per year (clue 2); a third is quarterly, with four copies a year (clue 4); and a fourth is bimonthly, with six copies a year (clue 8). These four figures add up to 74, so the remaining magazine must publish 26 copies a year; i.e., it is published biweekly. The least frequently published, the quarterly, isn't the science magazine (clue 4). Therefore, by clue 5, the literary journal is published biweekly, the gardening magazine monthly, the science magazine bimonthly and the fifth magazine is a weekly. The travel magazine isn't the weekly (clue 2) and must be the quarterly; the weekly, by elimination, deals with business. Two of the gift-givers are men, one of whom gave George the weekly (clue 2); that was not George's son (clue 3) and must have been his cousin, the only other relative mentioned who could be male. *Jornada* and *Quinta* were both gifts from women, and neither is the literary journal or the science magazine (clue 1); one is therefore the monthly gardening magazine and the other the quarterly travel magazine. George's son didn't give him the subscription to the

154

biweekly (clue 3), so another female relative did, and his son gave him the bimonthly science magazine. The latter is *Stratum* (clue 2). Now, by clue 6, *Quinta* is the monthly, and the subscription to the quarterly—which must be *Jornada*—was a gift from George's daughter. By clue 3, then, *Quinta* was a gift from George's sister, the biweekly the gift from George's niece. *Epitome* wasn't George's cousin's gift (clue 7), so it was from George's niece. The subscription from George's cousin, by elimination, was to *Aspect*. In sum:

> *Aspect,* business weekly: cousin
> *Epitome,* literary biweekly: niece
> *Jornada,* travel quarterly: daughter
> *Quinta,* gardening monthly: sister
> *Stratum,* science bimonthly: son

43. WEDDING BELLS

Allan and his bride were the first couple (clue 3), Miss Banks and her groom the third (clue 6). By clue 7, Miss Miller and Nancy and their grooms, in that order were either first and second or second and third. Miss Miller wasn't second (clue 4), so she was first and is married to Allan and Nancy was second. Since Mary is the female Andrews (clue 8), Nancy must be Miss Williams (clue 4), and she married Mr. Andrews. Mary Andrews and her groom were not last (clue 8); since Mary married John (clue 5), they can only have been the fourth couple. Karen was not married first (clue 1), second (Nancy Williams), or fourth (Mary Andrews), nor, since her maiden name is not Andrews (clue 8), was she married third (clue 1); Karen and her groom were the last to exchange vows, and John is Karen's brother; Karen's maiden name, by elimination, was Nelson. Mr. Banks, who didn't marry Karen (clue 8), must be Allan. By clue 2, then, Jean is Allan's sister and married Mr. Williams. Peter Miller (clue 9) can only be Karen's husband. Edward isn't Mr. Andrews (clue 5) and must be Mr. Williams. By elimination, Allan's wife is Ellen and Nancy's husband is David. In sum, in the order in which the couples exchanged vows:

> 1. Allan Banks & Ellen Miller
> 2. David Andrews & Nancy Williams
> 3. Edward Williams & Jean Banks
> 4. John Nelson & Mary Andrews
> 5. Peter Miller & Karen Nelson

44. JOBS AND HOBBIES

Ed is a photographer—either professional or amateur—and Barney is the other (clue 2). If Ed were the professional, Al would be the hobbyist (clue 1); so Barney is the professional, Ed the photo hobbyist. Similarly, both Charlie and Dick are outdoorsmen (clue 4)—but if Dick were the weekend camper, Al would be the forest ranger (clue 7); so Dick is the ranger and Charlie the weekend camper. We also know that Ed's occupation corresponds to Al's hobby (clue 1), Charlie's to Frank's hobby (clue 6), and Al's to Dick's hobby (clue 7); so Frank's occupation must correspond to Barney's hobby. Frank is a carpenter—either professional or amateur (clue 5). If that were his job, it would be Barney's hobby. One of the carpenters is a driver (clue 3), but we know Barney is a professional photographer, and Frank cannot be the weekend auto racer (clue 6). So Frank is the amateur carpenter who drives a cab—and Charlie is the professional carpenter (clue 6). Since Frank's occupation corresponds to Barney's hobby, Barney races cars as a hobby. Dick does not make jewelry (clue 8), so his hobby is electronics. Al is the TV repairman (clue 7). Jewelry making is Ed's occupation and Al's hobby. In sum, with occupation listed first:

> Al: TV repair, jewelry
> Barney: photography, racing
> Charlie: carpentry, camping
> Dick: forest ranger, electronics
> Ed: jewelry, photography
> Frank: cab driver, carpentry

45. TRUCKERS' LOADS

Two women are among the five, and one left her state of Pennsylvania with a load of leather (clue 3). She isn't Betty, who hauled only edibles (clue 11), so she is Lynn. One of the two women drove to Oklahoma (clue 1); it wasn't Lynn, who hauled leather (clue 4), so it was Betty. Only two edibles, peanuts and potatoes, are among the ten deliveries, so Betty hauled both of them; since peanuts weren't delivered to Oklahoma (clue 4), they were reloaded there, and Betty left her own state with potatoes. Lynn reloaded in Wisconsin (clue 6). Betty is mentioned in clue 1, and since Lynn is from Pennsylvania, the others mentioned in that clue are the three men: the one from New Mexico; John, whose first load was books; and the one from Indiana. Betty isn't from New York (clue 2), so John is, and Betty is from North Dakota. By clue 9, Rich is the one from Indiana; the one from New Mexico must be Wayne, and the latter's first load was lumber (also clue 9). Rich is then the one whose first load was electronic equipment (clue 6). Neither Lynn nor Rich reloaded with tires (also clue 6), nor did Wayne (clue 8); John's second load was tires. Lynn didn't haul cord or paper (clue 10), so her second load was fabricated metal. The lumber Wayne delivered wasn't exchanged for paper (clue 5), so he reloaded with cord, and Rich's second load was paper. By clues 1 and 7, only Wayne can be the one who drove to Wyoming. Paper wasn't reloaded in Iowa (clue 10), so tires were. Rich, by elimination, reloaded in Florida. In sum:

> Betty: N.D., potatoes, Okla., peanuts
> John: N.Y., books, Iowa, tires
> Lynn: Pa., leather, Wis., fabricated metal
> Rich: Ind., electronic equipment, Fla., paper
> Wayne: N.M., lumber, Wyo., cord

46. NECKLACE PENDANTS

None of the sunbursts were made of metal (clue 7). By clue 5, there were a total of five yellow sunbursts, two made of glass, so the other three were ceramic. Also by clue 5, Lea made three sunbursts that were not yellow, only one of them glass, so the other two sunbursts were ceramic. By clue 2, then, the remaining glass sunburst was red, the two ceramic ones orange. That takes care of all 8 sunburst pendants. By clue 1, there were a total of twelve yellow pendants. We know five were sunbursts. By clue 4, the remaining seven consisted of four stars and three moons, the latter three made of metal. Since just two of the yellow sunbursts were glass but there were a total of six yellow glass pendants (clue 1), the four yellow stars must all be made of glass. That takes care of all twelve yellow pendants. Now, eleven pendants were made of glass, six of them were yellow (clue 1), which leaves five to be red or orange glass stars or glass sunbursts (clue 3). Therefore, there were no glass moons. We have already ascertained the colors and materials of all the sunbursts, and only one was red glass and none was orange glass. The remaining four were stars and half were orange, so there were two orange glass stars and two red glass stars. That takes care of all eleven glass pendants. So far we have accounted for nineteen pendants, all of the yellows, all of the glass ones, and all of the sunbursts. Therefore, by clue 6, the six remaining pendants must be two orange ceramic moons, two orange ceramic stars, and two red metallic stars. In sum:

> Sunbursts: 2 orange ceramic, 1 red glass, 2 yellow glass, 3 yellow ceramic
> Stars: 2 orange glass, 2 orange ceramic, 2 red glass, 2 red metallic, 4 yellow glass
> Moons: 2 orange ceramic, 3 yellow metallic

47. THE EXERCISE REGIMEN

By the introduction, the women's heights are 5'2", 5'3", 5'4", 5'5", and 5'6". By clue 6, Gold is 5'6" tall, so she is either Mary or Phyllis. She lost twice as much as one of the others (clue 5). Each woman lost a whole number of pounds (clue 1), so Gold cannot be Mary, who lost 15 pounds; she must be Phyllis. By clue 2, Gomez is 5'2" tall, hence must be Mary. By elimination, the 5'3" woman must be Strasberg. By clue 4, the one who is 5'4" tall has lost more than 15 pounds and must be Brown. By elimination, Richards is 5'5" tall. Phyllis Gold

156

lost twice as much weight as Gladys (clue 5). Since Richards lost 10 pounds, Phyllis did not (clue 1), so Gladys is not Strasberg, who lost 5 pounds. We know that Brown lost more than 15 pounds; if she were Gladys, that would put Phyllis's loss at over 30 pounds—impossible, by clue 1. Thus, Gladys must be Richards, and Phyllis lost 20 pounds, so her original weight was 145 pounds. Since Brown lost 15 pounds more than one of the others (clue 4), and the other weight losses are all multiples of five, Brown's is also. By clue 1, the only possibility is that she lost 25 pounds, so she now weighs 115. She and Gladys Richards, who lost the 10 pounds, then weighed the same originally (clue 4), so Gladys now weighs 130. Erica, who now weighs 125 (clue 6), must be Strasberg, and she originally weighed 130. Brown, by elimination, is Lee. Mary Gomez originally weighed 120 (clue 3), so she now weighs 105. In sum:

First Name	Last Name	Height	Original Weight	New Weight	Number of Pounds Lost
Mary	Gomez	5'2"	120	105	15
Lee	Brown	5'4"	140	115	25
Gladys	Richards	5'5"	140	130	10
Phyllis	Gold	5'6"	145	125	20
Erica	Strasberg	5'3"	130	125	5

48. MOSQUITO PASS

Clue 1 lists all five men: Duke, Mr. Easton, Brazen's owner, Mistake's owner, and the winner. The team of Bronx and Queens didn't win (clue 2) and so must have belonged to either Duke or Mr. Easton. That team, though, finished just behind Zeke's (also clue 2), whereas Easton's was just behind Abner's (clue 5), so Duke owns Bronx and Queens. Conviction, which was a near burro, wasn't part of the winning team or Easton's (clue 5), so it belongs to Mistake's owner. Hotee, which wasn't paired with Brazen and didn't come in first (clue 3), can only be Mr. Easton's off burro. The off burro in last place wasn't Easton's Hotee or Abner's Ears (clue 5), Duke's Queens (clue 2), or Tripod (clue 3), so the team Conviction and Mistake was last. Zeke's team wasn't last (clue 2), nor was Abner's (clue 5), or Duke's Bronx and Queens (clue 2), and Jake doesn't own Conviction (clue 6), so only Ike can own the last-place team. Among the off burros, then, Duke owns Queens, Abner owns Ears, and Ike owns Mistake. Since Jake doesn't own Tripod (clue 6), Zeke must. By elimination Jake's off burro is Hotee, so he is Mr. Easton. Duke's Bronx and Queens did not win (clue 2). Abner's team placed just ahead of Jake Easton's (clue 5). Because Zeke's Tripod placed ahead of Easton's Hotee (clue 3), it must also have placed ahead of Abner's team, and only Zeke's team can be first. From clue 2, Duke's team Bronx and Queens was second and Norton's third; Norton can only be Abner and must be Brazen's owner (clue 1), and Brazen is then paired with Ears. Jake Easton's team, in fourth place, doesn't include Monument (clue 4), so Monument must be Zeke's nearside burro. By elimination, Shane is Hotee's partner. (Jake, who is fond of puns, refers to his team as Donkey Hotee and Donkey Shane.) Ike, whose team was last, is neither Weston nor Upton (clue 7), so he must be Sutton. Weston's team wasn't first (clue 3), so Weston must be Duke, and Upton is Zeke. In sum:

1. Zeke Upton's Monument and Tripod
2. Duke Weston's Bronx and Queens
3. Abner Norton's Brazen and Ears
4. Jake Easton's Shane and Hotee
5. Ike Sutton's Conviction and Mistake

49. SPIELBERG SATURDAY

Hank and Dawes saw, in some order, *E.T.* and *Back to the Future* for the second time (clue 3). The Edwards child saw *Close Encounters of the Third Kind* for the first time (clue 5). So, the pair of Andy and the Beech child, who each saw their movie for the third time (clue 1), must have seen *Raiders of the Lost Ark*. The pair of Kevin and Bob had each seen their movie at least once (clue 4), so neither of them was the Edwards child who saw *Close Encounters of the Third Kind* for the first time (clue 5); they saw either *E.T.* or *Back to the Future*. One of them had to be the Dawes boy mentioned in clue 3. Since Kevin saw his movie twice (clue 4), Bob must be Dawes and he saw his movie exactly once before (clue 3). Calvin, then, who saw *Back to the Future* (clue 5) must have paired with Hank, and Bob Dawes and Kevin saw *E.T.* By elimination, David Coombs paired with the Edwards boy to see *Close Encounters of the Third Kind*. The Edwards boy is not John (clue 6), so he is George and the Beech boy is John. Calvin must be the Ariso child (clues 5, 7). By clue 8, the Jeffers boy is Andy (clue 1). Hank is not Howe (clue 2) so Kevin is; and Hank is Peters. In sum, with the number of times that each boy had previously seen the movie in parentheses:

Calvin Ariso (0), Hank Peters (1): *Back to the Future*
John Beech (2), Andy Jeffers (2): *Raiders of the Lost Ark*
David Coombs (1), George Edwards (0): *Close Encounters*
Bob Dawes (1), Kevin Howe (2): *E.T.*

50. BABES

Four girls were born, and clue 3 lists them all, in birth order: the Larsons' daughter, Ann, and the Wilsons' twin girls. Mrs. Wilson is Trudy, and she named the first twin Jane (clue 6). Bob's wife had a girl (clue 2) who was born before Ann (clue 10), so he is Mr. Larson. Also from clue 2, Mr. Jacobs must be Ann's father, and George is Mr. Wilson. Jim also had a baby girl (clue 8), so he must be Ann's father, and the Larsons' baby is Jennifer (also clue 8). The second Wilson twin, by elimination, is Amy. We know the full names of all the girls' fathers, so boys were born to the Millers, Smiths, and Thompsons, and their fathers' first names are—in one order or another—Chuck, Gary, and Tom. Gary is not Mr. Smith (clue 1) or Mr. Thompson (clue 5), so he must be Mr. Miller. Nor is Tom Mr. Smith (clue 1); he is Mr. Thompson, and Mr. Smith is Chuck. The three mothers of boys are Mary (clue 5), Judy, and Carol (clue 7). Mary's husband is not Gary Miller or Tom Thompson (clue 5), so she is Mrs. Smith. Judy is not Mrs. Thompson (clue 7); she is Mrs. Miller, and Mrs. Thompson is Carol. Neither the Smiths' nor the Thompsons' son was born first (clue 1), nor was Judy Miller's boy (clue 9), so one of the girls was. From clue 3, that was Jennifer Larson, and from clue 8, the second baby born was Ann Jacobs. From clue 4, the Miller boy, who must be Andrew, was born third or fourth, and Richard was born fifth. We have been told the Wilson twins were born consecutively, so they can only have been born sixth and seventh. By clue 1, then, Andrew Miller was born third and the Smith boy—who must be Jason—fourth, and Richard is the Thompsons' son. Since the Larson girl was born first, Mrs. Larson is not Susan (clue 9); she is Betty, and Susan is Mrs. Jacobs. In sum, in order of birth from first to last:

Betty and Bob Larson: Jennifer
Susan and Jim Jacobs: Ann
Judy and Gary Miller: Andrew
Mary and Chuck Smith: Jason
Carol and Tom Thompson: Richard
Trudy and George Wilson: Jane and Amy

51. AIRLINE COUNTER

Clue 3 describes three travelers who stood in line consecutively—in order, the passenger for Atlanta, Alice, and Mr. Foley. If they were third, fourth, and fifth, that would mean the passenger for Dallas and Hall were respectively second and third, since there would be no other places for them (clue 4). Neither of the latter, by clue 4, is Tom; Tom would then be either first or last, contradicting clue 2. If we assume that those described in clue 3 were first, second, and third, one possibility would be that the passenger for Dallas and Hall were third and fourth—but again, Tom would have to be first or last. Another possibility would be that the passenger for Dallas and Hall were respectively fourth and fifth—i.e., that the five were, in order: the Atlanta passenger, Alice, Mr. Foley, the Dallas passenger, and Hall. Since

Tom is not one of the last two (again clue 4), nor is he first (clue 2) he would be Foley, and Elkins would be one of the first two in line (also clue 2); Elkins isn't Alice (clue 5) and so would be the Atlanta passenger. Then, by clue 1, the St. Paul passenger would be third and Alice's last name would be Dawes—but there would be no place for the Seattle passenger. So the only possibility remaining, from clue 3, is that the Atlanta passenger was second in line, Alice was third, and Mr. Foley was fourth. By clue 4, then, the Dallas passenger must have been Foley, while Hall was last in line—and since neither of the last two is Tom, Tom was second in line and Elkins was first (clue 2). Only two men are mentioned, so Mr. Foley is Bob. By clue 1, then, the St. Paul passenger was Alice, Tom's last name is Dawes, and Elkins was bound for Seattle. The latter is not Jean (also clue 1), so she is Lois, and Jean's surname is Hall. By elimination, Alice's last name is Girard and Jean Hall was bound for Chicago. In sum, in the order in which they waited in line:

> Lois Elkins, Seattle
> Tom Dawes, Atlanta
> Alice Girard, St. Paul
> Bob Foley, Dallas
> Jean Hall, Chicago

52. TOBY MUGS

Clue 2 tells us that Inez spent twice as much as the buyer of the Sherlock Holmes mug, who in turn spent $50 more than Hazel. The buyer of the Holmes mug was not Fran (clue 8), so she was Greta or Joan. By clue 5, Fran spent $50 more than the one who bought the Henry VIII mug. The latter was not Inez (clue 9); nor was she Hazel, since then Fran would have spent the same amount as the buyer of the Holmes mug (clue 4)—so the Henry VIII mug buyer was also either Greta or Joan, and clues 2 and 5 together describe all five buyers. Greta spent exactly $250 (clue 1). If she bought the Holmes mug, then, by clue 2, Hazel would have spent $200 and Inez $500. Since the total spent was $1300 (clue 1), and these three would add up to $950, that would leave $350 and, by clue 5, it would mean that Joan spent $150 for the Henry VIII mug and Fran spent $200. But that would make Fran's expenditure the same as Hazel's—again, contradicting clue 4. So Greta must have paid her $250 for the Henry VIII mug and, by clue 5, Fran spent $300. That leaves $750 of the $1300 to be divided according to the information in clue 2—i.e., the amount spent by Hazel, and that sum plus $50, and twice the latter (thus equal to twice what Hazel paid, plus $100), together add up to $750, or to put it mathematically, let X equal what Hazel paid, so $X + (X + \$50) + 2(X + \$50) = \$750$. When simplified, $4X + \$150 = \$750$ or $X = \$150$; so Hazel paid $150. Joan then paid $200 for the Holmes mug, and Inez spent $400. Hazel didn't buy the Ebenezer Scrooge (clue 3) or the Winston Churchill mug (clue 6); she bought the Shakespeare. The Scrooge mug wasn't Fran's (clue 7), so it was bought by Inez, and Fran bought the Churchill. In sum:

> Inez: $400, Ebenezer Scrooge
> Fran: $300, Winston Churchill
> Greta: $250, Henry VIII
> Joan: $200, Sherlock Holmes
> Hazel: $150, William Shakespeare

53. THE GARDENERS

Sarah received daffodils on either Monday or Tuesday (clue 8). Since she received violets on Tuesday (clue 4), she received the daffodils Monday, Tommy received daffodils Tuesday, and Kevin received violets on Thursday. Boys visited the daffodil-grower on consecutive days (clue 3), so Johnny received daffodils Thursday (when Kevin received violets), Kevin received them on Wednesday, and, by elimination, Betsy on Friday—the day Kevin received plum blossoms (clue 4). Johnny visited men Monday and Tuesday (clue 7); since he didn't receive daffodils until Thursday, neither Mr. Flowers nor Mr. Waters shared daffodils. Tommy visited Mr. Flowers on Tuesday, Wednesday, or Thursday (clue 1). Since Tommy received daffodils on Tuesday (clue 8—and Mr. Flowers doesn't grow daffodils), and visited a woman on Thursday (clue 7), he visited Mr. Flowers on Wednesday. Therefore, by clue 1, he visited Ms. Moss on Tuesday, and received the hyacinths on Thursday. Ms. Moss, then, shared the daffodils (to recap thus far) with Sarah on Monday, Tommy on Tuesday, Kevin on Wednesday, Johnny on Thursday, and Betsy on Friday. Since Johnny saw Mr. Flowers and Mr. Waters, in one order or the other on Monday and Tuesday (clue 7), and he did not visit Ms. Bloom on Wednesday (clue 2), he must have visited Ms. Gardner on Wednesday and Ms. Bloom on Friday (clue 7). We have established that Tommy received hyacinths (clue 1) on Thursday; since Tommy visited a woman on Thursday (clue 7), Mr. Waters did not share hyacinths. Kevin received plum blossoms on Friday (clue 4); he didn't see Mr. Waters on Friday (clue 6), so Mr. Waters didn't share plum blossoms either. Mr. Waters gave violets or tulips. Sarah visited Mr. Waters the day after Kevin did (clue 6); since she received violets on Tuesday (clue 4), two days *before* Kevin did, Mr. Waters didn't give violets; he gave tulips. Betsy received yellow flowers two days in a row (clue 5); only daffodils and tulips were yellow and she received daffodils Friday, so she received tulips from Mr. Waters on Thursday. Since we already know where all the boys were on Wednesday, and Betsy visited Mr. Waters on Thursday, Sarah visited Mr. Waters on Wednesday. Kevin, then, visited him on Tuesday (clue 6). By clue 7 then, Johnny visited Mr. Waters on Monday and Mr. Flowers on Tuesday. By elimination, Tommy visited Mr. Waters Friday, and Betsy visited Ms. Bloom Wednesday. Since Betsy visited Ms. Bloom on Wednesday, and we know where all the boys were on Tuesday, Sarah received her violets on Tuesday (clue 4) from Ms. Bloom. By elimination, Betsy visited Ms. Gardner on Tuesday. Since Mr. Flowers didn't give hyacinths (clue 1), he gave plum blossoms, and Ms. Gardner gave hyacinths, which Tommy received on Thursday. Kevin received plum blossoms from Mr. Flowers Friday (clue 4), so Sarah received hyacinths from Ms. Gardner on Friday and Kevin visited Ms. Gardner on Monday. Since Kevin visited Mr. Flowers on Friday and Betsy was at Mr. Waters's on Thursday, Sarah must have visited Mr. Flowers on Thursday while Kevin was visiting Ms. Bloom. By elimination, on Monday Ms. Bloom saw Tommy, and Mr. Flowers saw Betsy. In summary (with children listed in the order of their visits):

> Ms. Bloom, violets—Tommy, Sarah, Betsy, Kevin, Johnny
> Mr. Flowers, plum blossoms—Betsy, Johnny, Tommy, Sarah, Kevin
> Ms. Gardner, hyacinths—Kevin, Betsy, Johnny, Tommy, Sarah
> Ms. Moss, daffodils—Sarah, Tommy, Kevin, Johnny, Betsy
> Mr. Waters, tulips—Johnny, Kevin, Sarah, Betsy, Tommy

54.   COMMUNITY COLLEGE COURSES

By clue 2, the four women are Donna and Ms. Kane, who take only evening courses; Carolyn, who takes at least one daytime course; and the only one to take car maintenance, who also takes at least one daytime course. From clue 1, Ms. Jackson must be one of the latter two (since she isn't Donna); she takes one course with Donna, and another with Vicky, so she cannot be the only one to take car maintenance. Thus, she must be Carolyn. Carolyn's course with Donna must be an evening course (clue 2); Carolyn's second course, the one she shares with Vicky, must be a daytime course (also clue 2); therefore, Vicky must be the other daytime student in clue 2 who takes car maintenance. Vicky is not Ms. Kane (clue 2), Ms. Kane is Laura. Each woman is taking two courses. Vicky takes car maintenance by herself and another course with Carolyn Jackson, so she cannot be Ms. Moore who shares a class with Laura Kane. Ms. Moore can only be Donna; Vicky's surname, by elimination, is Wright. We know both Donna and Carolyn share both their courses with others, so the only one to take accounting, who also takes oil painting (clue 3), can only be Laura. Donna also takes oil painting (clue 4). By clue 5, aerobics, which meets only in the evening, must be the course taken by both Carolyn and Donna; the daytime course taken by both Carolyn and Vicky, by elimination, is decorating. In sum:

> Carolyn Jackson: aerobics, decorating
> Laura Kane: accounting, oil painting
> Donna Moore: aerobics, oil painting
> Vicky Wright: car maintenance, decorating

55. THE BABY-SITTER

We are given that LeAnn baby-sat for a total of 20 hours, 5 hours for one couple and a different amount of time for the other four couples. Clue 7 states that LeAnn baby-sat for Judy, who has only one child, for 3 hours. Judy's last name is not Truman (clue 1), McNeil (clue 4), Adelson (clue 5), or Brown (clue 6), so she is Mrs. Thompson. By clue 2, then, LeAnn sat for Gary and his wife for 6 hours. Since we know LeAnn sat for one couple for 6 hours, one for 5 and one for 3, in order to earn $20.00 she must have baby-sat one evening for 4 hours and another for 2. Therefore, the only possibility by clue 5, is that LeAnn sat for Carol for 4 hours and for the Adelsons for 2. Clue 6 states that Amy has more than one child and both Mark and the Browns have more than two children. Clue 1 states that both Bob and the Trumans have two children, and we know the Thompsons have one child. Therefore, Bob's last name is not Truman (clue 1), Adelson (clue 5), Brown (clue 6) or Thompson (clue 7); he is Mr. McNeil. Mark's last name is not Truman (clue 1), Brown (clue 6) or Thompson (clue 7); he is Mr. Adelson, who we know has three children (clue 5). So by clue 6, Amy has two children and Judy Thompson hired LeAnn on October 16th. Clue 3 states that John hired LeAnn on either October 2nd or 9th, and Sue hired her on either the 23rd or 30th. The McNeils hired LeAnn the weekend before Mary did (clue 4). Since we know Judy Thompson hired LeAnn on the 16th, there are only two possibilities for consecutive weekends, the 2nd and 9th, or the 23rd and 30th. If we assume Bob hired LeAnn on the 23rd and Mary on the 30th, Sue would then have to be Bob's wife. But Sue does not have precisely two children (clue 3) and Bob does (clue 1) so this is not possible. Therefore, Bob McNeil hired LeAnn on the 2nd, Mary did so on the 9th (clue 4). John must be Mary's husband, and Sue hired LeAnn on the 30th (clue 3). Mark Adelson, who we know hired LeAnn for 2 hours, is not married to Carol (clue 5) or Amy (clue 6) so he is Sue's husband. We know Gary is not Mr. Thompson (clue 2), so Paul is, and by elimination, Gary hired LeAnn for 6 hours on October 23rd. We know Carol hired LeAnn for 4 hours (clue 5), so she must be married to Bob McNeil. By elimination, Amy is Gary's wife. Amy's last name is not Brown (clue 6), so she is Mrs. Truman, and by elimination, Mary and John are the Browns, who hired LeAnn for 5 hours. In sum:

Oct. 2, Bob and Carol McNeil,   4 hrs.
Oct. 9, John and Mary Brown,   5 hrs.
Oct. 16, Paul and Judy Thompson,   3 hrs.
Oct. 23, Gary and Amy Truman,   6 hrs.
Oct. 30, Mark and Sue Adelson,   2 hrs.

56. BUS DRIVERS

Jane returned second (clue 4). The driver who returned last is not Lois (clue 2), nor Darlene or Charles (clue 3); Henry returned last. The driver who left first is not Lois or Henry (clue 2) nor Darlene or Charles (clue 3). Jane left first. The driver with 60 passengers is not Owens or King (clue 3) nor Newberry or Miller (clue 6). Lyons carried 60, and from clue 3 is not Darlene or Charles, neither of whom is Owens or King (clue 3). Darlene and Charles are Miller and Newberry. Since Newberry must be one of the five listed in clue 2 and is not Lois, Jane, Henry, or Miller, Newberry is the one with 50. Jane had 10 more students than Newberry (clue 4), so she had 60; no two carried the same number (clue 1), so Jane is Lyons and Henry had 55 (clue 4). We now know the number of students in three buses—50, 55, and 60. Three are also listed in clue 5: the driver who left second had 10 less than the driver who left third, who had 5 less than the one who returned third. With only five drivers, at least one from the first group must match up with one in clue 5. Jane, with 60, left first and returned second, so could not be any of the clue 5 drivers, nor could any of the drivers in clue 5 have driven 60 children (clue 1). If Newberry left second, the driver who left third would have duplicated Jane's 60. If Newberry left third, then the driver who returned third would have duplicated Henry's 55. Had Newberry returned third with 50, the driver who left second would have had 35, but from clue 1, all drivers had more than 35. Thus neither Jane nor Newberry is a clue 5 driver, so Henry is. Henry returned last. If he left third, the driver who returned third would have driven 60, but that's Jane's total and she returned second. Henry, then, left second with 55, the driver who left third had 65, and the driver who returned third had 70 (clue 5). Miller, with an odd number (clue 6), is not Henry (clue 2), so Miller had 65 and left third, and by elimination in clue 2, Lois had 70 and returned third. Lois is King or

Owens, neither of whom left last (clue 3); Lois left fourth and, by elimination, Newberry left last. Darlene didn't leave last (clue 7), so is not Newberry. Charles is Newberry and Darlene is Miller. Owens left before Darlene (clue 3), so Henry is Owens and Lois is King. Lois King returned after Charles (clue 3)—so Charles returned first and Darlene returned fourth. In summary:

	Left	Returned	# Students
Lois King	4	3	70
Jane Lyons	1	2	60
Darlene Miller	3	4	65
Charles Newberry	5	1	50
Henry Owens	2	5	55

57. PHYSICAL ACTIVITY CLASSES

Since none of the youngsters takes two courses the same evening (clue 1), the latest class Linda or Jane attends, as well as the earliest Bob or Rick attends, is Wednesday (clue 2). Bob and Rick cannot both take all their classes on Thursday and Friday, since Rick has a class the same night as Pete (clue 6); therefore either Bob or Rick has a Wednesday class. Jane, whose classes are not on consecutive evenings (clue 5), must attend classes Monday and Wednesday and by clue 2, her Wednesday class is at 6:00; her Monday class is then at 8:00 and the judo class at 6:00 that evening (clue 3). Linda's two classes are then Monday (the 6:00 judo class) and Tuesday, and Pete is the one who attends the other Tuesday class; Linda must be the one who is taking the balance-beam course (clue 6). Bob's classes, by clue 5, are either Wednesday and Thursday or Thursday and Friday; the latter is not possible, since that would leave no night on which Rick and Pete can both attend class (clue 6), so Bob's classes are Wednesday (at 8:00) and Thursday, Rick's Thursday and Friday, and by clue 6, Rick's Friday class is at 6:00, Pete's at 8:00. The karate class is at 6:00 on Thursday (clue 8). The floor-exercise class is either Wednesday or Thursday (clue 3). Rick's Friday class cannot be volleyball, squash, ballet (clue 4), tumbling, or handball (clue 9), so it is table tennis. Pete's class at 8:00 on Friday is not volleyball, squash, ballet (clue 4), or handball (clue 7), so it is tumbling. Nor can the Thursday-at-8:00 class be volleyball, squash, or ballet (clue 4), or floor exercise (clue 7), so it is handball; it is not Rick's class (clue 9), so it is Bob's, and Rick's is the 6:00 karate course. Floor exercise, by clue 3, is then Jane's 6:00 Wednesday course. The only remaining 6:00 class is on Tuesday, and must be squash (clue 10). Linda's balance-beam class is then at 8:00 and Pete takes the squash course. Jane's 8:00 class on Monday must be volleyball and Bob takes ballet (clue 4). In sum:

Mon.	judo, Linda	volleyball, Jane
Tues.	squash, Pete	balance beam, Linda
Wed.	floor exercise, Jane	ballet, Bob
Thurs.	karate, Rick	handball, Bob
Fri.	table tennis, Rick	tumbling, Pete

58. NEW FENCES

Clue 1 mentions three different fences, in decreasing order of length: the scalloped, the chain link, and the one on Tilmon Street. A fourth—like the one on Tilmon Street, shorter than the chain link—is the one erected by Sandy and her husband on Wright Street (clue 4). The fifth is the basket-weave fence on Elmer Street (clue 6). The stockade fence is not on Tilmon Street (clue 1); it is on Wright Street, and the one on Tilmon Street is the shadow box type. The shortest fence measures 70 feet and is the one erected by Joyce and her husband (clue 7); their fence is not the scalloped, chain link (clue 1), or basket weave (clue 6), so it is the shadow box on Tilmon Street. By clue 1, then, the chain link fence measures 140 feet and the scalloped fence 280 feet. By clue 4, the stockade fence on Wright Street is 125 feet long and Bob and his wife—by elimination, the couple on Elmer Street—needed 250 feet of fencing. The five fences in order of length are thus: scalloped, 280 feet; basket weave on Elmer Street (Bob and his wife), 250 feet; chain link, 140 feet; stockade on Wright Street (Sandy and her husband), 125 feet; shadow box on Tilmon Street (Joyce and her husband), 70 feet. Joyce's husband is not John (clue 3), Albert, or Warren (clue 8), and must be Greg. The longest, scalloped fence is not on Cline Street (clue 2); it is on Jay Street, and the chain link is on Cline Street. From clue 5, neither Michelle nor Lynn lives on Jay Street, and Michelle isn't the wife of Bob on Elmer Street, so Theresa lives on Jay Street, Michelle lives on Cline Street, and Lynn is Bob's wife. John must be Michelle's husband (clue 3). From clue 8, Warren is Sandy's husband and Albert is Theresa's. In sum:

> Theresa & Albert, Jay St.: scalloped, 280 ft.
> Lynn & Bob, Elmer St.: basket weave, 250 ft.
> Michelle & John, Cline St.: chain link, 140 ft.
> Sandy & Warren, Wright St.: stockade, 125 ft.
> Joyce & Greg, Tilmon St.: shadow box, 70 ft.

59.   BOOK BONANZA

By the introduction, a total of 45 books were read and each child read a different number; the only numbers meeting these conditions are one through nine. Among clues 5, 2, and 11 all nine children are mentioned. The three in the left row are Mary, the Peterson child, and the child who read two books (clue 5). The three in the middle row are Al, the Lotak child, and the child who read three books (clue 2). The three in the right row are Eleanor, the Fedirka child, and the one who read one book (clue 11). By clue 1, Larry can only sit in the middle or left row. He cannot sit in the middle row since his last name isn't Lotak (clue 7) and by clue 1, he read an even number of books; so he can only sit in the left row. The child who read only one book is in the right row, so Larry is not the one who read two books; he must be the Peterson child. The children who read one, two, and three books are—not necessarily respectively—Debbie, Regina and the Evans child (clue 9). According to clue 3, the Redeagle girl who read as many books as the two children behind her could not have read only three books, since the child who read two books is in the left row (clue 5) and the child who read one book is in the right row (clue 11). Since there are only four girls mentioned, the Redeagle girl is either Mary or Eleanor. In the three rows, three last names and the one-, two-, and three-book readers are accounted for (clues 2, 5, and 11), so the Adams child, who read four books (clue 8) and isn't Al (clue 7), must also be Mary or Eleanor. Since we already know that Mary (last name either Redeagle or Adams) and Larry Peterson sit in the left row, by clue 4, then, Bill, who sits in the same row as the Baer child, must be in the middle row and Fred, to Bill's right, in the right row. Since Fred isn't the Fedirka child (clue 7), he must be the child who read only one book, and his last name is Evans (clue 9). In the middle row, since the child who read three books is either Debbie or Regina (clue 9), Bill is the Lotak child. We know the one who read two books is also either Debbie or Regina, so Paul, who read seven books (clue 6), must be the Fedirka child. By clue 10, the Martin child who read three times as many books as the child in front of him/her, cannot have read three books since the child who read one book is in the right row (clue 11) and the one who read three is in the middle row (clue 2), so the Martin child cannot be either Debbie or Regina and must be Al. The Davis child isn't Debbie (clue 7); she is Regina, and Debbie's last name is Baer. Debbie Baer then, is the one who read three books, and sat in the middle row right behind Bill (clue 4); Al Martin sat behind her and read nine books (clue 10). Regina Davis is the child who read two books. Since Bill Lotak is in the first seat in the middle row, Fred Evans is in the first seat in the right row (clue 4). By clue 3, then, the Redeagle child is Mary and she sits in the first seat in the left row and Eleanor's last name is Adams and she read four books (clue 8). Since Larry read twice as many books as the person to his right (clue 1), he read six books and sits to Debbie's immediate left. Regina Davis, who read two books, sits in the last seat of the left row. Mary Redeagle then read eight books (clue 3). By clue 8, Eleanor Adams sits right behind Fred, and Paul sits behind her. By elimination, Bill read five books. In sum, front to back in each row:

Left row:	Middle row:	Right row:
Mary Redeagle, 8	Bill Lotak, 5	Fred Evans, 1
Larry Peterson, 6	Debbie Baer, 3	Eleanor Adams, 4
Regina Davis, 2	Al Martin, 9	Paul Fedirka, 7

60. FIVE WEDDINGS IN JUNE

By clue 7, Ms. Palmer was married either first or second. If she were married second and, by this same clue, Rebecca fourth, then, by clue 4, Paul—who, by clue 1, did not marry Ms. Palmer—could only have married third, and Rebecca's last name would be Akins. Therefore, Adam would have been married first or second (clues 1, 6), and the same would be true of Eric (clue 2), leaving Robert or Jason to marry Rebecca Akins, which contradicts clue 1 for Robert and clue 8 for Jason. So Ms. Palmer married first and Rebecca third. Now, by clue 4, Paul either married Rebecca or was married the week before her. Assuming the latter, by this same clue, Rebecca would again be Ms. Akins and Elaine would have married either fourth or fifth. Pam, too, would have married fourth or fifth (clue 1), and by clue 2, Jolene would have married Paul, and Eric would have married Ms. Palmer. But Rebecca Akins could not have married Adam, Robert (clue 1), or Jason (clue 8). Therefore, Paul married Rebecca, and by clue 4, Ms. Akins married fourth and Elaine fifth. Now, Eric married first or second (clue 2), as did Adam (clues 1, 6). Jason then married Elaine (clue 8), and Robert married Ms. Akins. Elaine's last name is not, then, Jabley or Everson (clue 1); it is Ranner. Elaine's maid of honor did not wear green (clue 5), so by clue 2, Eric married Ms. Palmer, Jolene married second, and Rebecca's maid of honor wore green. By elimination, Jolene married Adam. Jolene's surname isn't Jabley (clue 1), so Rebecca's is and Jolene is Ms. Everson. Ms. Akins isn't Anita (clue 1), so Ms. Palmer is and Ms. Akins is Pam. Now, by clues 1 and 9, Mr. Anson can only be Paul, and Pam carried violets. Elaine then carried daisies (clue 7). By clue 1, Mr. Ebert can only be Robert, Mr. Jilk must be Eric, and Mr. Rupert is Adam; Mr. Plahn, by elimination, is Jason. Rebecca Jabley didn't carry roses (clue 9) or lilies (clue 10); she carried carnations. Pam Akins' maid of honor didn't wear lavender or pink (clue 8); by clue 3, then, Elaine's maid of honor wore lavender, Anita's maid of honor wore blue, and Jolene carried lilies. It must have been Jolene's maid of honor who wore pink. By elimination, Anita carried roses, and Pam's maid of honor wore yellow. In sum, in the order married:

Eric Jilk & Anita Palmer: blue, roses
Adam Rupert & Jolene Everson: pink, lilies
Paul Anson & Rebecca Jabley: green, carnations
Robert Ebert & Pam Akins: yellow, violets
Jason Plahn & Elaine Ranner: lavender, daisies

61. THE MOUNTAINEERS

We know that the earliest expedition occurred in 1880; from clue 2, that group climbed the 20,702-foot peak. The highest peak mentioned, 26,660 feet, was scaled in 1953 (clue 5), and that was the last of the six expeditions (clue 10). The Canadian expedition was then in 1912 (clue 4). By clue 9, it was led by Howard and the 21,184-foot peak was scaled in 1898. Margherita was climbed in 1906 (clue 3). Now, we have five dates: 1880, 1898, 1906, 1912, and 1953. By clue 2, three of the expeditions took place at least 32 years after the first, so there was one between the 1912 and 1953 expeditions; i.e. the 1898 expedition was the second, the 1906 Margherita climb the third, and Howard's 1912 Canadian climb the fourth. Howard therefore ascended the 11,342-foot peak (clue 10). The expedition to the 26,391-foot peak was three years before Mr. Buhl's climb (clue 7); it can only have been the fifth one, occurring in 1950, and Buhl led the 1953 expedition. By elimination, Margherita's height is 16,795 feet. There is only one six-year gap between expeditions, so by clue 1, Luigi led the 1906 expedition, and Howard climbed Sir Sandford. Mr. Whymper then led the 1880 expedition (clue 12). In clue 2, Palmer can only be Howard. By clue 8, Conway climbed the Bolivian peak in either 1898 or 1906; he is not Luigi (clue 1), so he led the 1898 expedition. Luigi isn't Hertzog (clue 3), so Hertzog led the 1950 expedition and Luigi's surname, by elimination, is Amadeo. Hertzog is not Hermann's last name, although Hermann's was one of the last two expeditions (clue 6), so Hermann is Buhl. By clue 2, Maurice is Hertzog, and Hermann Buhl scaled the Pakistani peak. Edward isn't Conway (clue 14), so he is Whymper; Conway's first name, by elimination, is Martin. Neither Luigi (clue 1) nor Maurice (clue 13) went to Ecuador, so Edward Whymper did. Annapurna was one of the last two peaks climbed (clue 14), but not by Hermann (clue 6), so it was scaled by Maurice Hertzog. It is not in Uganda (also clue 6), so Margherita is. Hermann Buhl climbed Nanga Parbat (clue 8). Edward did not climb Illimani (clue 11), so Martin Conway did. By elimination, Edward Whymper climbed Chimbarazo, and Annapurna is in Nepal. In sum:

164

1880: Edward Whymper, Chimbarazo, Ecuador, 20,702 ft.
1898: Martin Conway, Illimani, Bolivia, 21,184 ft.
1906: Luigi Amadeo, Margherita, Uganda, 16,795 ft.
1912: Howard Palmer, Sir Sandford, Canada, 11,342 ft.
1950: Maurice Hertzog, Annapurna, Nepal, 26,391 ft.
1953: Hermann Buhl, Nanga Parbat, Pakistan, 26,660 ft.

62. BALLOON RACE

Neither the green and gold nor the blue and white balloon came in second (clue 1). The red and white balloon placed no better than fourth (clue 5), the green and red one no better than third (clue 6). The purple and gold one, therefore, placed second. Thus, by clue 2, which mentions all five balloons, George's balloon landed first, the balloon carrying the pilot's wife third, pilot Jones's balloon fourth, and the one in which Mr. Patterson was the passenger last. We are told one passenger was the pilot's mother (intro), another the pilot's wife (clue 2), and another was the pilot's fiancee (clue 3); the remaining two were a brother and a sister. Robert, the only male passenger (clue 4) must be Mr. Patterson, brother of the pilot. The pilot of the fifth-place balloon was then named Patterson as well. Pilot King, who is single and therefore not in the third balloon with his wife, did not place second (clue 1), so he must be George. Pilot Maloney didn't come in second (clue 8), so he placed third with his passenger Mrs. Maloney. The pilot of the green and gold balloon is not King (clue 1) and, since he is not married (also clue 1) didn't place third, and so, like the pilot of the red and white balloon, (clue 5) must have placed no better than fourth. The green and red balloon was not first (clue 6). Only the blue and white balloon could have placed first, and the green and red one must have placed third. By clue 6, then, Edward placed second and the passenger in George King's balloon was Baker. The fiancee's last name is Queen (clue 1). Since the second-place pilot of the purple and gold balloon is married (also clue 1), Queen can only be the fiancee of pilot Jones—who, again by clue 1, was in the green and gold balloon. Patterson was then the pilot of the fifth place red and white balloon. By elimination, Loomis was Edward's passenger—and since mother and son must have the same surname, this is the only pair which is possible; i.e., Edward's last name is Loomis, and his passenger was his mother. By elimination, George King's passenger was his married sister; her first name is Susan (clue 4). Patricia is married, but not to her pilot (clue 7), so she is Edward's mother. Esther isn't pilot Jones's fiancee (clue 1), so she is Mrs. Maloney, and Ms. Queen is Alice. Frank is married but is not Maloney (clue 8), so he is Patterson. Charles isn't pilot Jones (clue 3), so David is, and Charles is Maloney. In sum:

#1, George King: blue and white, sister Susan Baker
#2, Edward Loomis: purple and gold, mother Patricia Loomis
#3, Charles Maloney: green and red, wife Esther Maloney
#4, David Jones: green and gold, fiancee Alice Queen
#5, Frank Patterson: red and white, brother Robert Patterson

63. ICE-CREAM SURVEY

Six first names and four surnames are mentioned, so there is at least one set of siblings. The Brickel children, who ranked vanilla last (clue 5), are one such set. Irene has a brother who ranked chocolate last (clue 7), so they represent a second family, and the other two families involved are represented by single children. Of the siblings, one child in each family prefers a cone to a dish (clue 4), so Celia, who prefers a dish (clue 6), must be one of the Brickel children. Ivan is the only child who ranked strawberry first (clue 2), so Celia Brickel must have ranked chocolate first and strawberry second (clue 5). Her sibling, then, ranked strawberry first (clue 1), so he must be Ivan, and he ranked chocolate second; by clue 4, he prefers a cone. Since only Ivan ranked strawberry first, Irene's brother who ranked chocolate last must have ranked vanilla first and strawberry second. By clue 3, two children, Craig and a child named Rippel, had rankings that were identical. If they both ranked vanilla first, Irene and the sixth child would both have rated chocolate first (clue 1), vanilla second (clue 5), and strawberry last; this, however, would contradict clue 3. Clue 3 tells us that Craig's and the Rippel child's rankings were not the same as Celia Brickel's, so they can only have ranked chocolate first, vanilla second, and strawberry third. Since Craig ranked strawberry

165

last, he is not Irene's brother (clue 7), so he must be an only child and prefers a cone (clue 4). One of the two with identical rankings, however, prefers a dish and must be a sibling (clues 3, 4), so Irene must be the Rippel child who has the same rankings as Craig. She prefers a dish and so her brother prefers a cone (clue 4); the latter, by elimination, is Carl and the sixth child, also by elimination, is Iris. Craig's last name is Carmel and Iris's is Coffey (clue 3). Since only Ivan ranked strawberry first, and by clue 3, Iris's rankings were not identical to anyone else's, the only possibility is that she ranked vanilla first, chocolate second, and strawberry third; since she's an only child, she likes a cone (clue 4). In sum, with flavors listed in order of preference:

Celia Brickel: chocolate, strawberry, vanilla/dish
Ivan Brickel: strawberry, chocolate, vanilla/cone
Irene Rippel: chocolate, vanilla, strawberry/dish
Carl Rippel: vanilla, strawberry, chocolate/cone
Craig Carmel: chocolate, vanilla, strawberry/cone
Iris Coffey: vanilla, chocolate, strawberry/cone

64. TRUE-FALSE QUIZ

No two of the eight students answered the same number of questions. In order that they all receive the very same score, they must also have all gotten a different number of answers wrong. No student got more than seven wrong (clue 4). Thus, the eight students must have gotten, variously, seven, six, five, four, three, two, one, or none wrong. It also stands to reason that in order for all to receive the same score, those answering more questions would have more errors. Clue 11 tells us that Joe answered 28 of the 30 questions, but that at least one student answered more—i.e., 29 or 30. Let us assume that the student who answered 29 answered the most. If he or she had seven answers wrong, that student's score would have been $22-7$, or 15. Joe, then, would have had six wrong; but $22-6$ is 16, not 15. If we assume that one student answered 30 questions (and got seven wrong), a second answered 29 (and got six wrong), and Joe got five wrong, then the respective scores of those students would be 16 $(23-7)$, 17 $(23-6)$, and 18 $(23-5)$. Therefore, it must be assumed that one student answered 30 questions and got 7 wrong $(23-7=16)$ and that Joe, who answered 28, got 6 wrong $(22-6=16)$. Indeed, this works out if we assume continuing two-items-less answered and one more error in each case. Thus, the score all the students attained was 16, and the number of questions answered were, for the eight students, 30 (23 right, 7 wrong), 28 (22 right, 6 wrong), 26 (21 right, 5 wrong), 24 (20 right, 4 wrong), 22 (19 right, 3 wrong), 20 (18 right, 2 wrong), 18 (17 right, one wrong), and 16 (all right, none wrong). We know Joe is the one who answered 28 questions. By clues 9 and 11, Karen answered 26, the Clark girl answered 20, and the Horn youngster answered 18. Those who answered 30, 28, 26, or 24 questions all belong to the Drama Club, while the others do not (clue 3). By clue 6, Grace and the Leroy girl, who are in the Drama Club, answered fewer than the other two; they must have scored 26 and 24. The Leroy girl must be Karen who scored 26 and Grace scored 24. The first names mentioned include those of five boys and three girls; we have the scores of Karen Leroy, Grace, and the Clark girl, who are three different people; thus, Grace is the North girl (clue 7) and the Clark girl must be Dot. The ones who answered 22 and 20 questions are members of the Hiking Club, those who answered only 16 or 18 questions members of the Stamp Club (clue 10), and none belongs to both (clue 2). The one who answered 22 questions is the Evans boy, who belongs to the Model Railroad Club (clue 5), and he belongs to only those two clubs (clue 2). Since every student belongs to at least two clubs, and no two belong to exactly the same clubs, Dot Clark's second membership is in the Chess Club. By clue 8, the one who answered all 30 questions and Joe belong to the Model Railroad Club, while Karen and Grace belong to the Chess Club. Karen also belongs to the Hiking Club (clue 9). By clue 7, Mike is one of those who doesn't belong to the Drama Club, so Grace North belongs to three clubs; since they must be different from Karen's, Grace's third club is the Stamp Club. Mike then belongs to only the Hiking and Model Railroad Clubs, therefore he is the Evans boy. The one who answered 16 questions and got them all correct isn't Paul or Al (clue 1) and must be Bill. Since Joe belongs to the Model Railroad Club in addition to the Drama Club, the Horn boy also belongs to the Model Railroad Club—and since the Horn boy belongs to the Stamp Club, so does Joe (clue 11). Bill's second club is then, to be different from the Horn boy, the Chess Club. Paul and the Fisher boy together represent all five clubs, so one must belong to the Drama Club, and they have no memberships in common (clue 7). Paul cannot be Horn, since the Fisher boy would be either Joe or the one who answered 30 questions, and all three belong to the Model Railroad Club. Paul must be the one who answered 30 questions, while the Fisher boy is Bill. Paul, then, must also belong to the Hiking Club. The Horn boy, by elimination, is Al. By clue 1, Joe's last name is Ross and Paul's is Mills. In sum, in order of the number of questions answered (with the number right/wrong for the score of 16):

> Paul Mills, 30 (23/7): Drama, Model RR, Hiking
> Joe Ross, 28 (22/6): Drama, Model RR, Stamp
> Karen Leroy, 26 (21/5): Drama, Chess, Hiking
> Grace North, 24 (20/4): Drama, Chess, Stamp
> Mike Evans, 22 (19/3): Hiking, Model RR
> Dot Clark, 20 (18/2): Hiking, Chess
> Al Horn, 18 (17/1): Stamp, Model RR
> Bill Fisher, 16 (16/0): Stamp, Chess

65.   PETS ALLOWED—NO VACANCY

Cathy Burk and her husband live in apartment 2C (clue 6). By clue 3, the Fields must be in apartment 2B, Phil and Kate in 3B, and Gina and her husband in 1B; either Mike and his wife or the couple who own Cleo the cat live in 2A, and the same is true of 2C. Bob and Ann on the second floor, who own a dog (clue 2), can only be the Fields. By clue 1, the Carters and their bird can only live in apartment 1A; Kim and her husband in 2A; and George is Gina's husband, and their pet's name is Twinkle. We are told that no two couples on the same floor or in the same vertical line have the same kind of pet, so Kim and her husband have a cat, and Twinkle is also a cat. The couple in 3A then have a dog, Kate and Phil a bird, the couple in 3C a cat, the Burks a bird, and the couple in 1C a dog. By clue 3, Kim's cat is Cleo, and Cathy's husband is Mike. The couple in 3A are the Davises, and the dog in 1C is Tiny (clue 2). By clue 4, Marie and her husband can only live in 3C, Kate's and Phil's last name is Mills, and the Burks' bird is Peppy. By clue 5, since Tom's pet, Fluffy, isn't a dog, Tom can only be Marie's husband, and Jim and his wife, with their pet named Chipper, can only be the Carters. Now, by clue 7, Martha can only be Mrs. Davis, and Kim's last name is Jones. Sally isn't Tiny the dog's owner (clue 8), so Sue is, and Sally is Mrs. Carter. Sue isn't Mrs. Harris (clue 2), nor are the Harrises Marie and Tom (clue 5), so they are Gina and George. Marie and Tom aren't the Adamses (clue 4); they are the Willises, and the Adamses are Sue and her husband. Pete isn't Kim's (clue 1) or Martha's husband (clue 7); he is Sue's. Mr. Davis isn't Tim (clue 2), so Mr. Jones is, and Mr. Davis is Tony. Peanuts isn't the Davises' or the Fields' pet (clue 2) and must be the Millses' bird. The Davises' pet isn't Pepper (clue 7), so Pepper is the Fields' dog, and the Davises' dog is Frenchie. In sum:

> 3A: Martha & Tony Davis, dog Frenchie
> 3B: Kate & Phil Mills, bird Peanuts
> 3C: Marie & Tom Willis, cat Fluffy
> 2A: Kim & Tim Jones, cat Cleo
> 2B: Ann & Bob Field, dog Pepper
> 2C: Cathy & Mike Burk, bird Peppy
> 1A: Sally & Jim Carter, bird Chipper
> 1B: Gina & George Harris, cat Twinkle
> 1C: Sue & Pete Adams, dog Tiny

66.   HOMECOMING DAY

Jay, first in line, graduated in 1946 (clue 1). The teacher, fifth in line, graduated in 1956 (clue 6). By clue 8, no two of the five graduated the same year or in consecutive years—but each graduate's time at the college overlapped that of the adjacent person in line by at least a year. This would not have been true at this four-year college if they had graduated four years apart—so the interval between graduation years of adjacent people in the line was, in every case, either two or three years. The second person in line then must have graduated in 1943, 1944, 1948, or 1949; the fourth must have graduated in 1953, 1954, 1958, or 1959. The graduation year of the third person, between these two, must be both two or three years after the second and two or three years before the fourth. This is possible only if the second in line graduated in 1948 or 1949; the third in line, in 1950, 1951, or 1952; and the fourth, in 1953 or 1954. The first graduation year, then, was 1946, and the latest 1956. By clues 2 and 4, there are two five-year intervals between graduation years. This is possible only if the third person in line graduated in 1951. We now have the following, in chronological order (and in line order, as well): 1946, 1948 or 1949, 1951, 1953 or 1954, and 1956. By clue 3, Dot graduated four years after Jackson. There is only one possible four-year interval: Jackson graduated in 1949, Dot in 1953. The teacher who was fifth in line wasn't Rose (clue 6) or Sam (clue 7) and must have been Carl. The 1951 graduate is then the lawyer (clue 2). The other five-year interval is described in clue 4: the lawyer is Irons, and 1946 graduate Jay is an engineer. Carl, fifth in line, is neither Larsen (clue 2) nor Hollis (clue 5); he is Kalb. Nor can Hollis be Dot (again, clue 5), so she is Larsen, and Hollis is Jay's last name. Sam is lawyer Irons, and Jackson is the physician (clue 7); by elimination, Jackson's first name is Rose, and Dot Larsen is a banker. In sum, from first to fifth in line:

> Engineer Jay Hollis, 1946
> Physician Rose Jackson, 1949
> Lawyer Sam Irons, 1951
> Banker Dot Larsen, 1953
> Teacher Carl Kalb, 1956

67. FROM CORDIALITY TO FRIENDLYTOWN

We are told there were four occasions on which one car passed another (intro). By clue 3, the woman driving the blue car was in the lead for part of the trip but was neither the first to leave Cordiality nor the first to arrive in Friendlytown; thus, at least one car passed her at some point. By clue 2, Ms. Lyons was the first to leave Cordiality but was next-to-last to arrive in Friendlytown, so she was passed by three cars. This then accounts for the four passings: Ms. Lyons was passed by three of the four cars behind her, including the blue one, and the woman in the blue car was passed exactly once. Therefore, the woman in the blue car passed *only* Ms. Lyons. If the former had been the third to leave Cordiality, she would have had to pass more than one car in order to take the lead for part of the trip—so she must have been second to leave, and hers was the first car to pass Ms. Lyons. The car that left Cordiality last cannot have arrived at Friendlytown first, since it would have had to pass four cars to do so, giving us too many passing events. If, after the woman in the blue car passed Ms. Lyons, the car that left Cordiality next-to-last had passed the three leading cars and arrived in Friendlytown first, Ms. Lyons would have arrived in Friendlytown third rather than next-to-last. Therefore, the car that arrived in Friendlytown first was the third to leave Cordiality, and it must have passed both Ms. Lyons and the blue car at some point, accounting for two more passings. And in order for Ms. Lyons to arrive in Friendlytown next-to-last, the fourth car to leave Cordiality must have passed her as well. The last car to leave Cordiality did no passing, then, and was also the last to arrive in Friendlytown; it was the tan one (clue 1). Now, to determine the order of the second, third, and fourth passings. After the blue car passed Ms. Lyons, it was in the lead and Ms. Lyons was second. The next car to pass another cannot have been the next-to-last, since that would have made it impossible for the third car to gain the lead going into Friendlytown; therefore, the second passing was by the third car, which passed Ms. Lyons, moving her into third place, and this was the second passing event. That car did not continue ahead to pass the blue car at this point, since the second and third passings were done by two different cars (clue 4). The third passing, then, took the original next-to-last car in front of Ms. Lyons, into third place, moving her into next-to-last place. Finally, the car that left Cordiality third, now in second place, passed the blue car and took the lead going into Friendlytown, while the blue car arrived second. Remember, Ms. Lyons was passed by three different cars. We have already established that the blue car did the first passing and that the third car to leave Cordiality did the second passing and that the fourth car to leave Cordiality did the third passing. Ms. Nichols did either the second or third passing (clue 4). She wasn't fourth leaving Cordiality (clue 5) so she left third and did the second passing and the cream-colored car (clue 4) did the third passing. Ms. Lyons didn't drive the gray car (clue 2), so Ms. Nichols did. Mr. O'Brien didn't drive the tan car (clue 1), and the blue one was driven by a woman (clue 3), so his was the cream-colored one. By elimination, the woman driver of the blue car was Ms. Palmer, the tan car was driven by Mr. Moore, and Ms. Lyons' car was red. In sum, in order of leaving Cordiality, with position of arrival in Friendlytown in parentheses:

Ms. Lyons, red car (4th)
Ms. Palmer, blue car (2nd)
Ms. Nichols, gray car (1st)
Mr. O'Brien, cream car (3rd)
Mr. Moore, tan car (5th)

—and the four passing events, in chronological order: (1) Palmer passed Lyons; (2) Nichols passed Lyons; (3) O'Brien passed Lyons; (4) Nichols passed Palmer.

68. HOME IMPROVEMENTS

By clue 4, the house at #107 is buff. By clue 3, a second house is yellow and is the home of the Geller family. By clue 5, two of the other three houses are white. By clue 7, the fifth house is red. By clue 6, the Gellers do not live at 101, and, by clue 2, neither do the Longs. Suppose that #101 is the home of either the Holts or the Jensens. Then #105 would be the home of the other of those two families (clue 3). Since the house at #107 is buff, the Gellers' yellow house would have to be #103 (again, clue 3). The Kilmers, by clue 1, could not live at #109 and would live at #107 and the Longs, by elimination, at #109. The Kilmers would be the ones who added a garage (clue 2). By clue 5, the house at either #101 or #109 was white, so the only other house that could also be white is #105. The red house would be at one end or the other, so the attic finishing would have to have been done by the family at #105 (clue 7). Thus, the house to the other side of the Kilmers, at #109, would be the white house where a family room was added (clue 1). By elimination, the kitchen refinishing would have to be the improvement of either the Gellers or the family at #101, contradicting clue 6. We began by eliminating the Gellers (clue 6) and the Longs (clue 2) from living at #101, and by assuming #101 to be the home of either the Holts or the Jensens; since it cannot be, it must be the home of the Kilmers. Thus the house at #103 is a white house where a family room was added (clue 1). By clue 5, the second white house cannot be #101 and must be #109. The Gellers' yellow house can only be #105. By elimination, the red house is #101 and the attic finishing at #105 (clue 7). By clue 8, the Holts do not live at #103; by clue 3, then, they must live at #107 and the Jensens at #103. By elimination, the house at #109 is the Longs' and the Holts added a garage (clue 2). The Longs must have redone their kitchen (clue 6), and, by elimination, the Kilmers added central air-conditioning. In sum:

101, red: Kilmers, air-conditioning
103, white: Jensens, family room
105, yellow: Gellers, attic
107, buff: Holts, garage
109, white: Longs, kitchen

69. ACADEMIC GRANTS

Mary was awarded the largest amount, $3500 (clue 2). Since no two recipients are the same age (intro), there is one of each of the ages 17 through 24. The 23-year-old received $1000, the 20-year-old, $1750, and Mandy $2000 (clue 12). The 21-year-old received more than $3000 (clue 10). Ms. Vail, age 22, cannot possibly have received as much as $1000 (clue 4). Mandy is at least 21 years old (clue 3) but since she received $2000 (clue 12), she cannot be exactly 21 (clue 10). Nor can she be 22 (clues 4, 12) or 23 (clue 12), so she is 24. By clue 3, then, the psychology major is the 22-year-old Ms. Vail and Ms. Mack is the 20-year-old (clue 3) who received $1750 (clue 12). No two received the same amount—so Mary, who received twice as much as Ms. Mack, cannot be the physics major (clue 11). Nor is Mary's field history (clue 1), math (clue 4), psychology, since that's Ms. Vail's field, who received less than $1000, art (clue 6), English (clue 7), or engineering (clue 9), so it is music. Ms. Mack, who received the $1750, then majors in English (clue 7). The one who received the least is not the student of history (clue 1), math (clue 4), art (clue 6), electrical engineering (clue 9), or physics (clue 11), so she is psychology major Vail. Mary's age must be either 19 or 21 (clue 2). From clue 8, Ms. Jones is at least 21, but she is not 24, since we know the psychology major is 22; nor can she be 23, since that would make Candy 19 and Mary would then be 21 and would be the physics major—while we know that in fact she is the music major. So Ms. Jones must be 21 and, from clue 8, the physics major is 19 and Candy

17. Music major Mary is then Ms. Jones, and the physics major is Ms. Cole (clue 2). By clue 10, then, the $1750 recipient is Jean, and Ms. Vail received only $250. Therefore, by clue 4, the math major received $500 and the 23-year-old $1000 recipient is Amy. We now know the first names of the 23- and 24-year-olds, so Nikki is the 22-year-old Ms. Vail and 17-year-old Candy's surname is Smith (clue 5). 23-year-old Amy received $1000 (clue 12). Since the math major received less than Amy (clue 4), the math major is not 24-year-old Mandy who received $2000 (also clue 12). We also know the majors of the 19-, 20-, 21- and 22-year-olds, so the math major is either 17-year-old Candy Smith or the 18-year-old. Thus far, we know six of the eight amounts—$3500, $2000, $1750, $1000, $500, and $250—and we know that none of them represent Ms. Cole who is the physics major or Ms. Smith. By clue 1, then, the amounts received by Ms. Nelson and Ms. Lind must be represented in the amounts mentioned above and therefore can only be $1000 and $500 respectively, while the history major received $1500. Since this is a seventh amount, Ms. Smith must be the history major and physics major Cole then received $3000 (clue 11). Mandy, by elimination, is Ms. Fox, so Amy Nelson's major is art and Ms. Lind's first name is Barbara (clue 6). By elimination, Ms. Cole's first name is Debra and Mandy's field is electrical engineering. In sum:

> Mary Jones, 21, music: $3500
> Debra Cole, 19, physics: $3000
> Mandy Fox, 24, elect. engineering: $2000
> Jean Mack, 20, English: $1750
> Candy Smith, 17, history: $1500
> Amy Nelson, 23, art: $1000
> Barbara Lind, 18, math: $500
> Nikki Vail, 22, psychology: $250

70. BATTER UP

We are told the nine boys all had different numbers of home runs, as well as different numbers of strike-outs, in both cases ranging from one to nine. Shortstop Ed Price had five home runs and eight strike-outs (clue 3). The three basemen are Mike, Billy, and Steve (clue 1). Matt is neither the pitcher nor an outfielder (clue 4) and must be the catcher. Robby, who isn't an outfielder (clue 2), is then the pitcher and the three remaining boys—Jim, Joey, and Tim—are the outfielders. The three basemen's home runs totaled nine (clue 1). The three numbers can only be one, two, and six or two, three, and four; in either case, the boy who had two home runs is one of the basemen. Tim, an outfielder, can only have had one, three, or four (clue 6), and the same is true of outfielder Joey (clue 8)—but if one of these boys had one and the other three or four, that would eliminate both sets of possibilities for the three basemen. Therefore, Tim must have three home runs and Joey four, or vice versa, while the boys who had six home runs and the one who had only one were both basemen. By clue 2, the Stone boy had two more home runs than pitcher Robby, who had six more than the Lentz boy—so the Stone boy had nine and Robby seven, while the Lentz boy is the baseman who had only one. Since the Stone boy with nine home runs, also by clue 2, isn't the catcher, he is the last outfielder, Jim, and catcher Matt, by elimination, had eight home runs. Remember the basemen scored 1, 2, and 6 home runs. By clue 4, then, the baseman who had two home runs is the Day boy, who is not Steve; nor is he Mike (clue 1), so he is Billy. The Lentz boy who had one home run isn't Mike (clue 2), so he is Steve, and Mike is the baseman who had six home runs. Since Tim and Joey each had either three or four home runs, by clues 6 and 8, catcher Matt's last name is either Miller or Hoyt, as is baseman Mike's. By clue 5, the Burk boy had nine strikeouts and the Moore boy four. Remember that Ed Price had eight. By clue 4, the only possibility is that Billy Day had seven and Jim Stone two. Now, by clue 2, pitcher Robby had three more strike-outs than Mike, who had one more than Steve Lentz; Robby can only have nine strike-outs and must be the Burk boy, while Mike had six strike-outs and Steve Lentz five. Mike with six strike-outs, is the first baseman (clue 1), while Steve Lentz plays third base and Billy Day second base (clue 2). The Moore boy isn't Tim (clue 5), so he is Joey. Since Joey Moore had four strike-outs, by clue 6, Tim must have had three strike-outs, and Jim Stone plays center field. Tim cannot then have had three home runs (clue 1); he had four, and Joey had three. The Miller boy is then catcher Matt (clue 6), while Mike's surname is Hoyt. By elimination, Tim's last name is Sand and Matt Miller had one strike-out. Tim Sand plays left field, Joey Moore right field (clue 7). In sum:

170

Robby Burk, pitcher	7	9
Billy Day, 2nd base	2	7
Mike Hoyt, 1st base	6	6
Steve Lentz, 3rd base	1	5
Matt Miller, catcher	8	1
Joey Moore, rt. field	3	4
Ed Price, shortstop	5	8
Tim Sand, left field	4	3
Jim Stone, ctr. field	9	2

71. BILLY AND THE PETS

There are fifteen cats and six dogs, twenty-one pets in all among the six families, and each
has at least one. The family with the most pets has two more than the one with the second
most (clue 3), who in turn have two more than Billy's family, which has three or more (clue
5). If the family with the most had nine, that would total twenty-one for these three families
alone; if the family with the most had eight, that would mean a total of eighteen, and since a
fourth family would have two (also clue 5), that would leave only one pet for the other two
families. Therefore, the family with the most pets has seven, another family has five, Billy's
family has three, and precisely one family, by clue 5, has only one (since it refers to *the*
family with the fewest). That leaves five for the last two families, so one of them has two pets
and the other has three. Billy has two dogs (introduction), one brown and one white (clue 8).
Four other families have dogs (clue 2), so Billy's third pet must be a cat. The litter of five
black kittens and their mother must belong to the family with seven pets. From clue 1, four
cats—two black males and two orange cats—live at one house, so they must belong to the
family with five pets. The family with seven pets and the family with five pets live as far
apart as possible (clue 3), so they must live at 101 Maple Street and 106 Elm Street or at 105
Maple Street and 102 Elm Street. The family which owns the litter's father and grandmother
are adjacent to the family with the litter (clue 9), so they are *not* the family with five pets and
must have a total of two or three pets, of which one at most is a dog, so they are not Billy's
family. The Smiths, who own only one kitten, plus at least one other pet of the same color,
but none of any other color (clue 6), are thus also owners of either two or three pets. We
have thus far established that the family with seven pets has five black kittens; the family
with five pets owns two orange cats and two black male cats; a family with two or three pets
owns the litter's father and grandmother; and the Smiths (who may or may not be the latter
family) own one kitten. That makes twelve cats. The three remaining cats are the Jacksons'
orange male, which is not among those owned by the family with five pets (clue 1), the
Bakers' gray male (clue 7), and a calico cat (clue 8). The last is the only one which can be the
litter's mother, and the family which owns her and her litter also has a white dog (also clue
8). We know they are not the Smiths, Jacksons, or Bakers; they are not the Kings, who own
a red dog (clue 6), nor are they the Allens (clue 4), so they are the Canfields. Four families
have at least one black cat or kitten (clue 2). We know two of those are the family with seven
pets and the family with five. We know of two other black cats, the litter's father and
grandmother (clue 9), so theirs is the third family. The color of all the other cats is accounted
for except the kitten owned by the Smiths, so their kitten is black and they are the fourth
family. Since the Smiths have more than one black pet (clue 6), they must also own the only
black dog mentioned, the black puppy (clue 7), making them the family with two pets. The
litter's father and grandmother must then belong to a family with three pets. Since we have
placed cats with five different families, the family with one pet owns only a dog (clue 2). The
only cats not placed yet are the orange one owned by the Jacksons and the gray one which
belongs to the Bakers. Since Billy owns a cat, his name is either Jackson or Baker. We know
the Canfields live in a corner house. Billy lives next door to them (clue 8), so he lives at
either 103 Maple Street or 104 Elm Street; in either case, his family has three adjacent
neighbors. The Bakers have only two and must live on a corner (clue 7). Thus, Billy's family
is the Jacksons, and they have an orange cat. The Canfields' back-fence neighbors are the
three-pet family who own the litter's father and grandmother (clue 9); the Bakers are *not*
adjacent to the Canfields (clue 7). The Bakers are adjacent to the Smiths and since they own
a cat, they are not the family with one pet. Thus, the Bakers must be the family with five
pets, all cats. All the other families own dogs (clue 2). Since the Kings have a red dog (clue

171

6), the Allens must have the collie. We know the Bakers and the Canfields live as far apart as possible. The Bakers live on Elm Street (clue 7), so the Canfields live on Maple, at 101 or 105. They do not live at 105 (clue 9), so they live at 101 and the Bakers at 106 Elm Street. We know that Billy Jackson's family lives next door to the Canfields, so the Jacksons live at 103 Maple Street. We also know that the three-pet family with the litter's father and grand-mother lives adjacent to the Canfields, so they live at 102 Elm Street. The Allens and their collie and the Smiths with their black puppy are both adjacent to the Bakers at 106 Elm Street (clue 7), so the Kings and their red dog live at 102 Elm, and the Allens are the one-pet family. The latter do not live at 104 Elm Street (clue 4), so they are at 105 Maple and the Smiths at 104 Elm. In sum:

> MAPLE STREET
>> 101, Canfields: 5 black kittens, calico cat, white dog
>> 103, Jacksons: orange cat, white dog, brown dog
>> 105, Allens: collie
> ELM STREET
>> 102, Kings: 2 black cats, red dog
>> 104, Smiths: black kitten, black puppy
>> 106, Bakers, 2 black cats, 2 orange cats, gray cat

72. BIGFOOT AND UFOs

Clues 3 and 6 differentiate the nine team members: Richie, Grange, and the pitcher all believe Bigfoot is a primitive man; Evers, Mike, and the right fielder all think Bigfoot is a large animal; Fulton, Les, and Oscar all think Bigfoot is a hoax. We are told that no two of the players agree completely, so within each of these groups of three, there are three different opinions about UFOs. The shortstop takes the middle position on both questions (clue 8), so he is one of the second group of three—i.e., either Evers or Mike. The right fielder doesn't believe that UFOs contain aliens (clue 2), so he is the one of that group who believes they are a hoax. None of the three basemen thinks either phenomenon is a hoax (clue 1), so none are in the last group of three; one must be the third member of the second group, so one of the basemen believes UFOs contain aliens, while the other two basemen are among those who think Bigfoot is a primitive man—one taking the position that UFOs contain aliens, the other that they are a natural phenomenon. The pitcher, then, believes that UFOs are a hoax. The group that thinks Bigfoot is a hoax then consists of the other two outfielders and the catcher; the catcher, by clue 2, is the one of the group who believes UFOs contain aliens. So, then, do Adams and Sam, by clue 4—and since Sam isn't Grange, he must be Evers, while Adams is Richie. Grange and Mike, then, both believe that UFOs are a natural phenomenon, and Mike is the shortstop. We know the right fielder thinks UFOs hoaxes. By clue 9, then, the left fielder thinks they are a natural phenomenon (and the center fielder thinks them hoaxes), while the third baseman is in total disagreement with both of them and can only be Richie Adams. By clue 5, third baseman Adams is also in complete disagreement with Brown and Oscar, and we know Oscar is one of those who think Bigfoot a hoax, so Brown is one of those who think Bigfoot a large animal and, since he is not the right fielder (also clue 5), he is Mike. And since he thinks UFOs are a natural phenomenon, Oscar must think them a hoax and is the center fielder. We know the three who think UFOs a natural phenomenon are Grange, Mike Brown, and the left fielder; by clue 7, Grange's first name is Ken and Harris is the left fielder, while Fulton, who is not Oscar (clue 6), is the catcher. The latter, we know, believes UFOs contain aliens and Bigfoot is a hoax. By the second part of clue 9, then, the second baseman cannot be Sam Evers, who agrees with Fulton on UFOs, and must be Ken Grange; Sam Evers, by elimination, is the first baseman, and Phil can only be the right fielder. By the second part of clue 7, then, Ned is the pitcher, Clark is Phil, and Iles is Oscar. By elimination, Ned's last name is Drake, and Fulton's first name is Tony. In sum, with the opinion on UFOs first in each case:

> Richie Adams, 3rd base: aliens, primitive
> Mike Brown, shortstop: natural, animal
> Phil Clark, right field: hoax, animal
> Ned Drake, pitcher: hoax, primitive
> Sam Evers, first base: aliens, animal

172

Tony Fulton, catcher: aliens, hoax
Ken Grange, second base: natural, primitive
Les Harris, left field: natural, hoax
Oscar Iles, center field: hoax, hoax

73. ZIONSBURG NEIGHBORS

As indicated, there are two homes facing in each direction, and only those facing north or south can lie "between" two others as defined. Thus, by clue 3, lots #2, #3, #6, and #7 are owned (not necessarily respectively) by David, Mr. King, Fred, and Ms. Jones. Since four men and four women are mentioned, the four corner homes are then occupied by one man and three women. These are the four which are located as far apart as possible, so by clue 4, their owners are Mr. Owens, Ms. Powers, the potato grower (who must be a woman), and Betty. Adam, whose house faces north, #2 or #3 or south, #6 or #7 (clue 11), can only be Mr. King; Mr. Owens' first name must be George. Lots #2 and #3, with the houses facing north, are both owned by men (clue 2) who must be David and Adam King, so Mrs. Jones's home must face south; by the same clue, she is then the cabbage grower. Since she lives between two men (clue 3), the one man who occupies a corner home, George Owens, must also live on the south side of the block—i.e., he owns lot #5 or #8. The man on the other side of Ms. Jones must be Mr. Queen (clue 2), and by clue 3, his first name is Fred. David's last name, by elimination, is Macy. Either David Macy or Adam King owns the plum tree (clue 2); i.e., that tree is on either lot #2 or lot #3. By clue 9, the peach tree, the apple tree, and the pear tree are on three lots in a row, so they can only be on the south side, and one of the corner lots on that side—#5 or #8—has either a peach tree or a pear tree. We know Ms. Jones's house faces south, and she raises cabbage; she isn't Carol (clue 1). Helen's house faces east (clue 2), and we know Betty lives in a corner house, so Ms. Jones must be Edna. Helen's east-facing house (clue 2) must be a corner lot, so she is therefore either Ms. Powers or the potato grower (clue 4); in either case, by clues 1 and 12, she cannot own either a pear tree or a peach tree. The other east-facing house belongs to a person who raises peas (clue 2)—who, again by clue 12, also cannot own a pear or peach tree. Therefore, the pear and peach trees are, in one order or the other, on lots #5 and #7, and the apple tree is on lot #6. By clue 2, the west-facing corner lots #1 and #5 are occupied by Ms. Nelson and the iris grower; those on the east-facing corner lots #4 and #8 are Helen and the person who raises peas. These four are, in one order or another, Mr. Owens, Ms. Powers, Betty, and the potato grower (clue 4). Helen, then, must be either Ms. Powers or the potato grower. Clues 1 and 12 eliminate the potato grower from being the owner of lot #5 who has a tree beginning with the letter "p." Since Betty is as far as possible from the potato grower (clue 4), this eliminates Betty from lot #4. According to clue 1, of the people mentioned in clue 4, only Betty or Mr. Owens can raise the peas on lots #4 or #8. We've already established that Betty cannot live on lot #4 and that Mr. Owens lives on lot #5 or #8, so the pea grower, either Betty or Mr. Owens, lives on lot #8, and Helen (clue 2) lives on lot #4. Since peas are grown on lot #8, according to clue 4, Betty cannot be the woman who owns corner lot #1 (clue 4); that woman must be Carol. We know the plum tree is on lot #2 or #3, the tree on lot #5 is either a peach or a pear, as is the one on lot #7, and the apple tree is on lot #6. The lemon and orange growers whose homes face in the same direction (clue 7) can only be those whose homes face east. The cherry tree isn't Carol's (clue 1)—so it, like the plum, is on lot #2 or lot #3, and Carol's tree is the apricot. Adam King doesn't own the cherry tree (clue 11), so David Macy does, and the plum tree is Adam's. David then raises lettuce (clue 2). Remember that Helen is *either* Ms. Powers or the potato grower. Clue 10 lists all four who live on the north side, and we know that Carol has an apricot tree and David Macy raises lettuce. Thus, David must also grow roses, while Adam King raises either tomatoes or beans, as does Helen. Helen is thus Ms. Powers. By clue 4, then, George Owens owns lot #5, so the grower of peas is Betty; by the same clue, Carol grows potatoes. By clue 3, then, Edna Jones owns lot #6, Fred Queen lot #7. By clue 6, we can now place David Macy at lot #3; Fred Queen grows zucchini, and his is the pear tree, while George owns the peach. Lot #2 is then Adam King's, so Carol grows gladiolas (clue 11). Since Carol's and George's homes face west, Carol is Ms. Nelson, and George raises irises (clue 2). Betty's last name, by elimination, is Long—so the orange tree is hers and the lemon tree Helen's (clue 1). Cabbage-grower Edna Jones doesn't grow camellias or carnations (clue 12), so by clue 8, the carnation grower must be Betty, while Fred grows camellias. The tulip grower raises neither beans (clue 5) nor tomatoes (clue 12) and can only be Edna. Marigolds are grown by a woman (introduction), so she must be Helen, and Adam raises daffodils. He then raises tomatoes, and Helen grows beans (clue 5). By elimination, George grows asparagus. In sum:

#1, Carol Nelson: apricot tree, gladiolas, potatoes
#2, Adam King: plum tree, daffodils, tomatoes
#3, David Macy: cherry tree, roses, lettuce
#4, Helen Powers: lemon tree, marigolds, beans
#5, George Owens: peach tree, irises, asparagus
#6, Edna Jones: apple tree, tulips, cabbage
#7, Fred Queen: pear tree, camellias, zucchini
#8, Betty Long: orange tree, carnations, peas

74. CHRISTMAS AT THE JOHNSONS'

We know that each member of the family received a gift from each of the other five, one each day Monday through Friday. The only identical gifts were bathrobes and sweaters, received by all the children (clue 10); these were from their parents (clues 6, 20). Since Mrs. Johnson gave gifts to the boys Monday and Tuesday (clue 13), and no one received a sweater on Monday (clue 2), the bathrobes were from her and the sweaters, given Tuesday through Friday, from Mr. Johnson, who must have given his wife her gift Monday. Bathrobes and sweaters are the only items of clothing mentioned, except a shirt which Dad received (clue 17), and the bathrobes were handmade (clue 1), so the gift Jane received Thursday was the sweater from her father (clue 8). Jane received bubble bath from Jill on Friday (clue 16), so she must have received her bathrobe Wednesday. Jim gave a gift of golf balls on Wednesday (clue 3), to his father (clue 17). Since Mr. Johnson received his gift from Jane Monday (clue 4), and a tie from one daughter two days before the gift from his wife (clue 12), the last two can only have been the tie from Jill on Tuesday and the gift from his wife on Thursday. Mom then gave Jill her bathrobe on Friday, and Mr. Johnson's gift on Friday, by elimination, was from John. Jim's Friday gift of a baseball, which was not to his mother (clue 3), can only have been to John, while John received the sweater Friday, and Jane's Friday gift was to her mother. We have already established that Jill gave Dad a tie on Tuesday, so her gift to John two days before she gave one to her mother (clue 14), can only have been Monday and Wednesday respectively; Thursday, by elimination, she gave Jim his gift. The boy who received the bathrobe Monday was then Jim, while John received his Tuesday. We have accounted for Jane's and Jim's sweaters, and for the gift John received Tuesday, so the one who received the sweater on Tuesday was Jill, and John received his on Wednesday. That accounts for all the gifts John received except the one from Jane, so he must have received that on Thursday. Since we know Jill's Tuesday gift was from her father, Jane gave Jill her present on Wednesday, and, by elimination, to Jim on Tuesday. The gift Jim received Wednesday, by elimination, was from John. We know that on Wednesday, John received a sweater and Jane a bathrobe, so Jim received a softball and Jill a doll (clue 15). Monday, when Jim received his bathrobe, John received a model car (clue 9). Jill's gift of a poster was then to Jim (clue 11), and the boy who received the puzzle Thursday (clue 5) was John. Jim then received the magic set on Tuesday, while Jane received the Monopoly game on Monday (clue 19); it wasn't from Jim (clue 3), it was from John and Jim's necklace, by elimination, was given to Jill. The gift Jane received on Tuesday can only have been from Jim, and so it was hairbrushes (clue 3); his gift to his mother was then on Thursday, and was the plate (also clue 3). By elimination, John's gifts Tuesday and Thursday were respectively to his mother—earrings (clue 18)—and Jill. Mrs. Johnson received perfume from a child (clue 18), so the purse and candle, which she received in that order two days apart (clue 7), must have been received Monday from her husband and Wednesday from Jill, while the perfume was from Jane. We know Mr. Johnson received a tie and golf balls, and from whom. The other gifts he received were a cribbage board, which was not from Jane (clue 4), a shirt, and aftershave lotion (clue 17). Only the shirt can have been from his wife (clue 1), so the aftershave was from Jane and the cribbage board from John. The one remaining gift, the bracelet, was by elimination John's gift to Jill. In sum:

	Dad gave	Mom gave	Jane gave	Jill gave	Jim gave	John gave
Mon.	Mom purse	Jim bathrobe	Dad aftershave	John model car	Jill necklace	Jane Monopoly

Tues.	Jill sweater	John bathrobe	Jim magic set	Dad tie	Jane brushes	Mom earrings
Wed.	John sweater	Jane bathrobe	Jill doll	Mom candle	Dad golfballs	Jim softball
Thurs.	Jane sweater	Dad shirt	John puzzle	Jim poster	Mom plate	Jill bracelet
Fri.	Jim sweater	Jill bathrobe	Mom perfume	Jane bubble bath	John baseball	Dad cribbage bd.

75.   THE MERCHANTS' CHRISTMAS DECORATIONS

From clue 2, four merchants want each design, and each of the four who want each design wants it in a different color—a total of sixteen different combinations, one for each of the sixteen stores; the owner of the hardware store at #10 wants silver wreaths. Therefore, all the merchants on the south side want gold or silver, and all those on the north side want red or green (clue 1). The owner of the luncheonette at #8 (clue 9) wants a gold design (clue 7). The owner of #6 wants silver (clue 10), as do the owners of #2 and #4 (clue 3); therefore, the owners of #12, #14, and #16 want gold. The owners of #2 and #4 do not want stars (clue 3), so it is the owner of #6 who wants silver stars. The four corner establishments are the florist, the vegetable store, the butcher, and the bank, in one order or another (clue 6). The stationery store is not next to the hardware store but is closer to it than the drugstore is (clue 13); this could not be true if the drugstore were at #6 or #14, so the drugstore is at #4, the shoe store at #3. The toy store and the deli are, in one order or the other, at #7 and #9 (clue 9). The children's clothing store is between the toy store (clue 5) and an adult clothing store (clue 12), so it is on the north side. Therefore, the deli is at #7, the toy store at #9, the children's clothing store at #11, and the adult clothing stores at #13 and #14 (clue 4). The owner of #13 wants green (also clue 4). The stationery store must be at #6 (clue 13). The owner of the shoe store wants wreaths (clue 11). The merchants at #5 and #7 want different colors (clue 10), as do those at #7 and #9 (clue 7) and #9 and #11 (clue 5); i.e., two of these four want red and two want green. Since the owners at #1 and #3 want different colors (clue 3), as do the owners of #1 and #15 (clue 6), then the owners at #1 and #13, want the same color, which we know is green—so those at #3 and #15 want red. Since the shoe-store owner wants red wreaths, the merchant at #15 cannot. The owner of the vegetable store, which we know is at a corner, wants wreaths and is next to the women's clothing store (clue 14); the vegetable store is then at #16 and the women's clothing store at #14 (and the men's clothing store at #13). The florist is at #1 (clue 6). The butcher doesn't want silver (clue 8), so by clue 6, the butcher is at #15 and the bank is #2. The butcher disagrees on color with the luncheonette owner and so, by clue 8, must agree on that point with the bookstore owner. The latter must be at #5 and want red. By elimination the fish store is at #12. By clues 10, 7, and 5, the deli owner then wants green, the toy-store owner red, and the owner of the children's clothing store green. Those at #1 and #2 don't want stars (clue 3), so the butcher does (clue 6); so, then, does the luncheonette owner (clue 8). By clue 7, then, #9 cannot have a star; it is then the one at #11 who wants stars (clue 5). The fish store's owner who wants gold agrees with the bookstore owner (who wants red) on design and doesn't want bells (clue 8); since we have placed the gold star and the red wreath preferences, they both want festoons. Since we have accounted for three designs in red, the toy-store owner wants bells; the deli owner then wants festoons (clue 7). Since we have placed the other three gold preferences, the merchant at #14 wants bells. Only green bells and wreaths remain to be placed. Since #16 wants a gold wreath, by clue 6, the florist wants green bells and the owner of the bank wants silver festoons. By elimination, the druggist wants silver bells and the owner of the men's clothing store wants green wreaths. In sum:

#2:	bank, silver festoons		#1:	florist, green bells
#4:	drugstore, silver bells		#3:	shoestore, red wreaths
#6:	stationery store, silver stars		#5:	bookstore, red festoons
#8:	luncheonette, gold stars		#7:	deli, green festoons
#10:	hardware store, silver wreaths		#9:	toy store, red bells
#12:	fish store, gold festoons		#11:	children's clothing, green stars
#14:	women's clothing, gold bells		#13:	men's clothing, green wreaths
#16:	vegetable store, gold wreaths		#15:	butcher, red stars